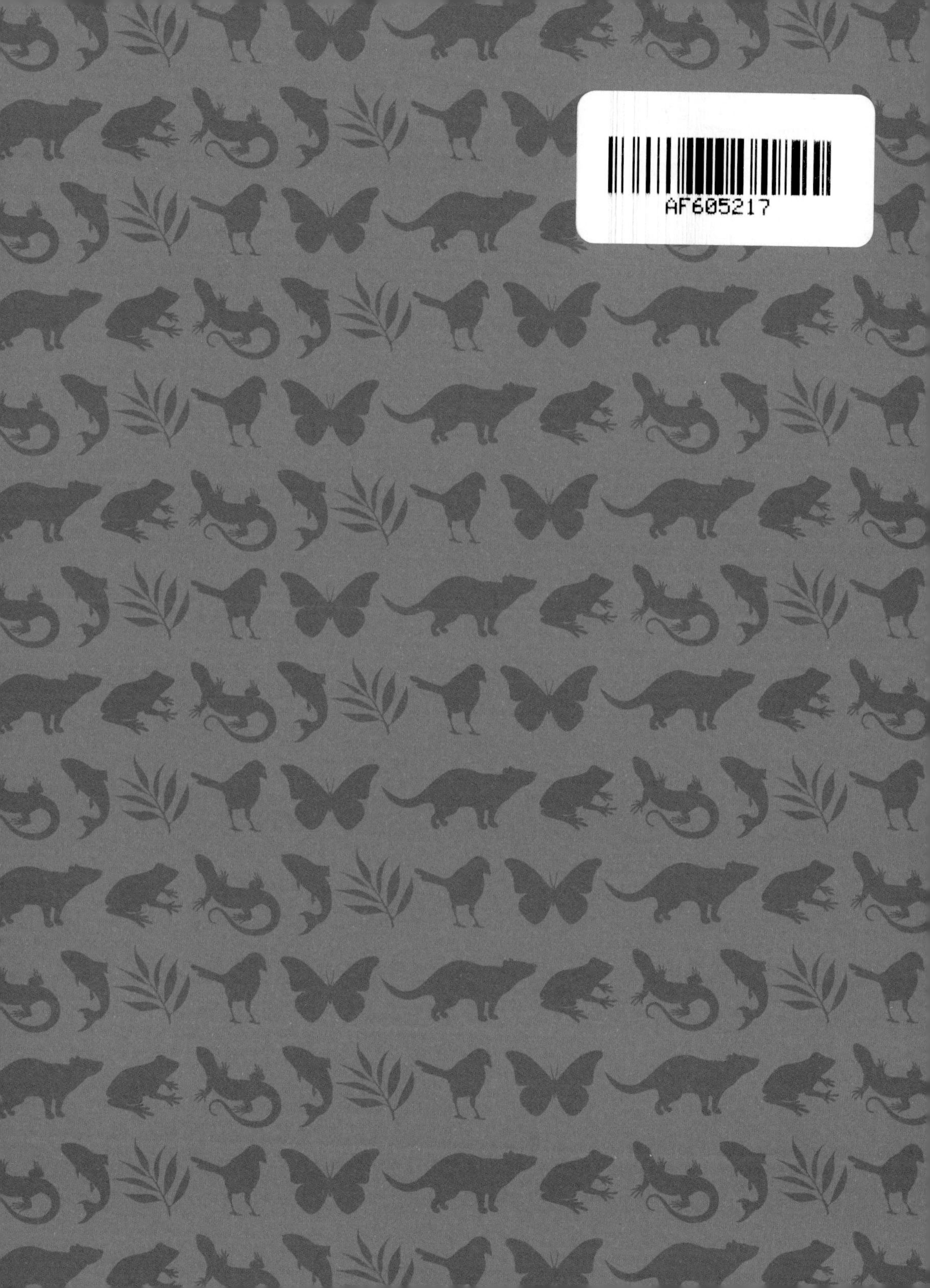
AF605217

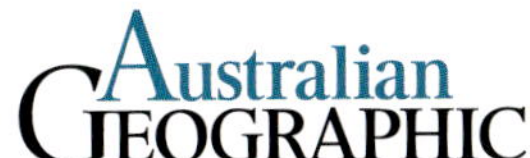

Extraordinary & Endangered

Thank you to the NSW Government Saving our Species Program for partnering with us on this very special book. Without you it would never have been made. We would also like to express our gratitude to all the incredible contributors to this project. Your thought-provoking photographs, hours in the field, dedicated study and relentless passion give us hope for the future, and for all of earth's species and habitats. Together we can turn the tide.

In the spirit of reconciliation, Australian Geographic acknowledges the Traditional Custodians of Country throughout Australia, and their continuing connections to land, sea and community. We pay our respects to their Elders past, present and emerging, and extend that respect to all Aboriginal and Torres Strait Islander Peoples today.

Cover: Greater Glider (*Petauroides volans*)
Named Grevillea, this female greater glider was found as a baby when some trees were cut down in Condamine, Queensland, as part of a mining operation. Rescued as an orphan and hand raised, she was unable to be released back into the wild, so was later moved to live at Currumbin Wildlife Sanctuary.

Given their high dependence on forest and large hollow-bearing trees, habitat destruction and fragmentation through deliberate tree clearing, as well as the impacts of climate change and bushfires, pose the greatest threats to these wonderful animals. Once ruling our tree tops along the east coast of Australia, glider populations have crashed by about 80 per cent in just the last 20 years, so sadly these magnificent animals are now listed as vulnerable to extinction.
Words and photograph: Doug Gimesy.

Contents

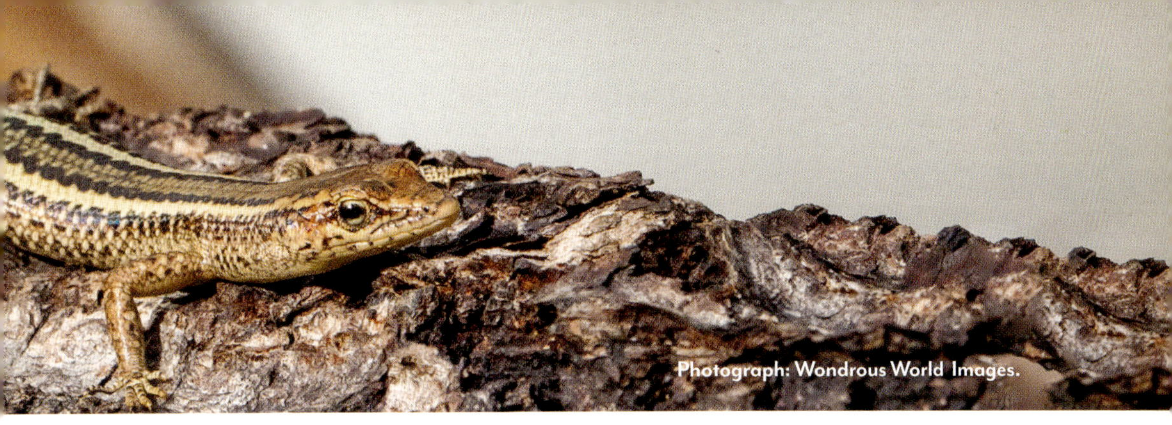

AMPHIBIANS

INVERTEBRATES

ALGAE, FUNGI & PLANTS

Foreword

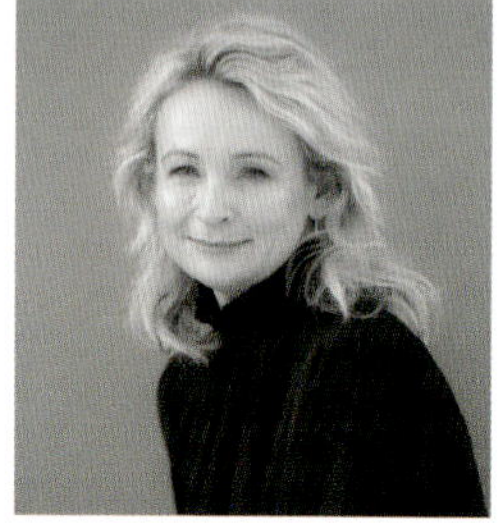

FOR MORE THAN 36 YEARS, Australian Geographic has documented Australia's flora, fauna, people, places and culture through our award-winning bimonthly magazine and other publishing channels. The Australian Geographic Society, our charitable arm, provides practical and financial support to Australian conservationists. It has donated hundreds of thousands of dollars to assist Australians working tirelessly to protect native species as they battle multiple threats including climate change, habitat destruction and feral invasive species.

Over time we have witnessed many tragic extinctions as plants and animals are pushed to the brink. I won't quote the statistics here; they are frightening, and you will read about some of them in this book.

The truth is we live in unprecedented times. Unpredictable weather patterns driven by anthropogenic climate change are leading to more frequent and more destructive bushfires, longer and more severe droughts, and life-threatening floods. Unabated population growth compounds these impacts on our already critically challenged environment, and the flora and fauna that depend on it for their survival.

This book does not aim to be the definitive list of all the species we are about to lose; sadly that list is much longer than the 100 unique species documented here. Rather, it is a tribute to the passionate, dedicated people who work tirelessly to try to save them. Among them are conservationists, scientists, photographers, wildlife rescuers and many ordinary Australians. These are the people on the frontline. They are leading the charge and fighting the good fight, but they cannot do it alone. The problem has grown too big, it is too important, and it has reached a stage that is beyond critical.

I hope this book will help illuminate a problem that is much greater than most people realise, and put a face to some of the species we stand to lose. Here you will also find hope and, hopefully, the resolve to act and become part of the solution.

Our role at Australian Geographic is to do what we do best – document what is happening through expert storytelling and powerful photography, in the hope that we can inspire change, raise awareness, and celebrate the extraordinary beauty of this country of ours and the fragile, beautiful, unique living things that we share it with.

Jo Runciman,
Managing Director, Australian Geographic
Member of the board of trustees,
Australian Geographic Society

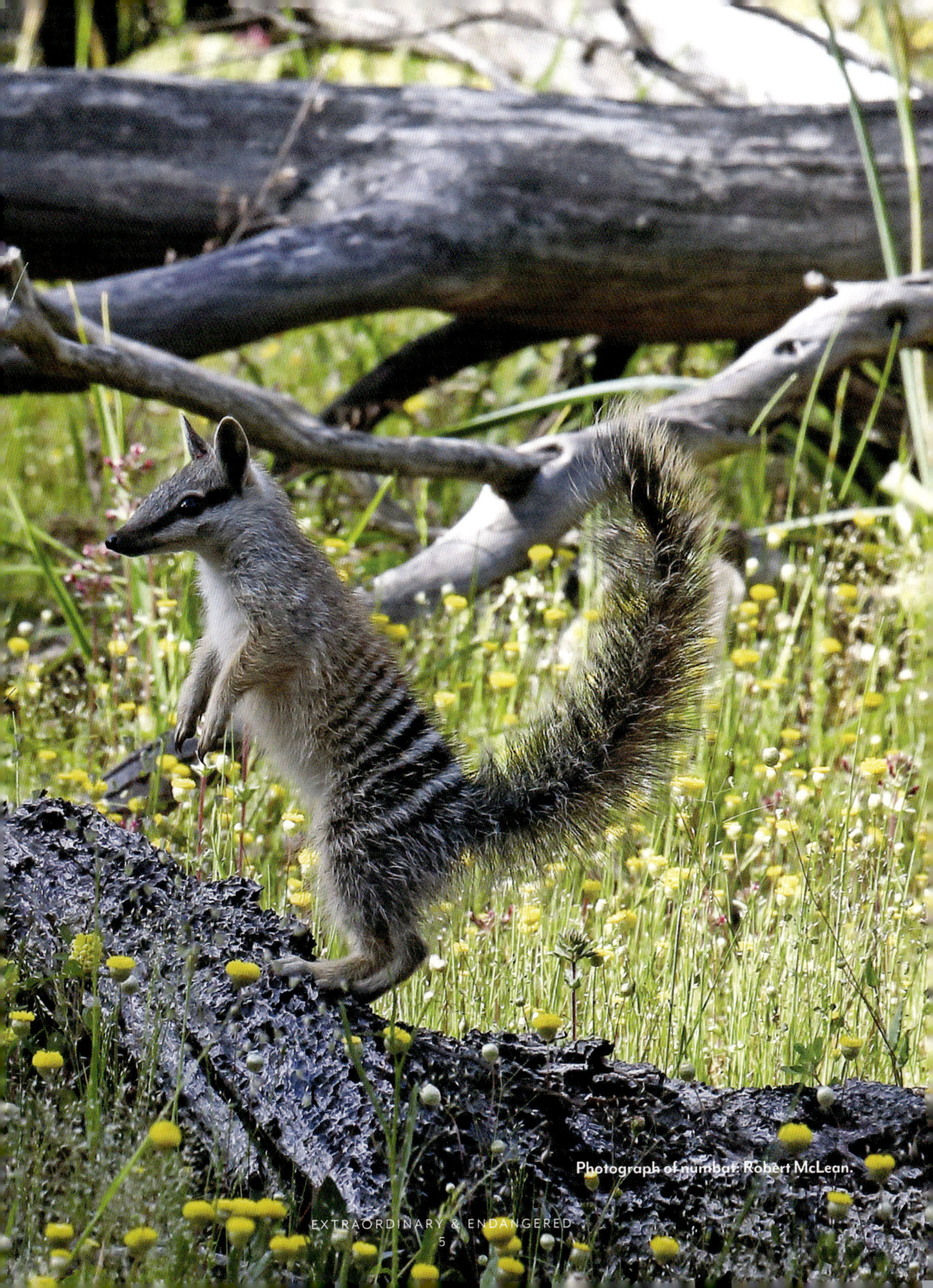

Photograph of numbat: Robert McLean.

Tasmanian Devil

Sarcophilus harrisii

The world's largest surviving marsupial carnivore, the Tasmanian devil was once found on Australia's mainland, but it is now only present in Tasmania.

One key threat to this special species is devil facial tumour disease (DFTD) – an infectious cancer that only affects Tasmanian devils. DFTD is transmitted through biting, fighting, and mating, and is one of the only cancers known to spread like a contagious disease. Tasmania's habitats will suffer enormously should the devil – a keystone species – become extinct.

Work is currently underway to save the species in Tasmania, and there's also an effort to reintroduce the species to mainland Australia to function as the apex predator it once was.

Words: Tim Faulkner.
Photograph: Aussie Ark.

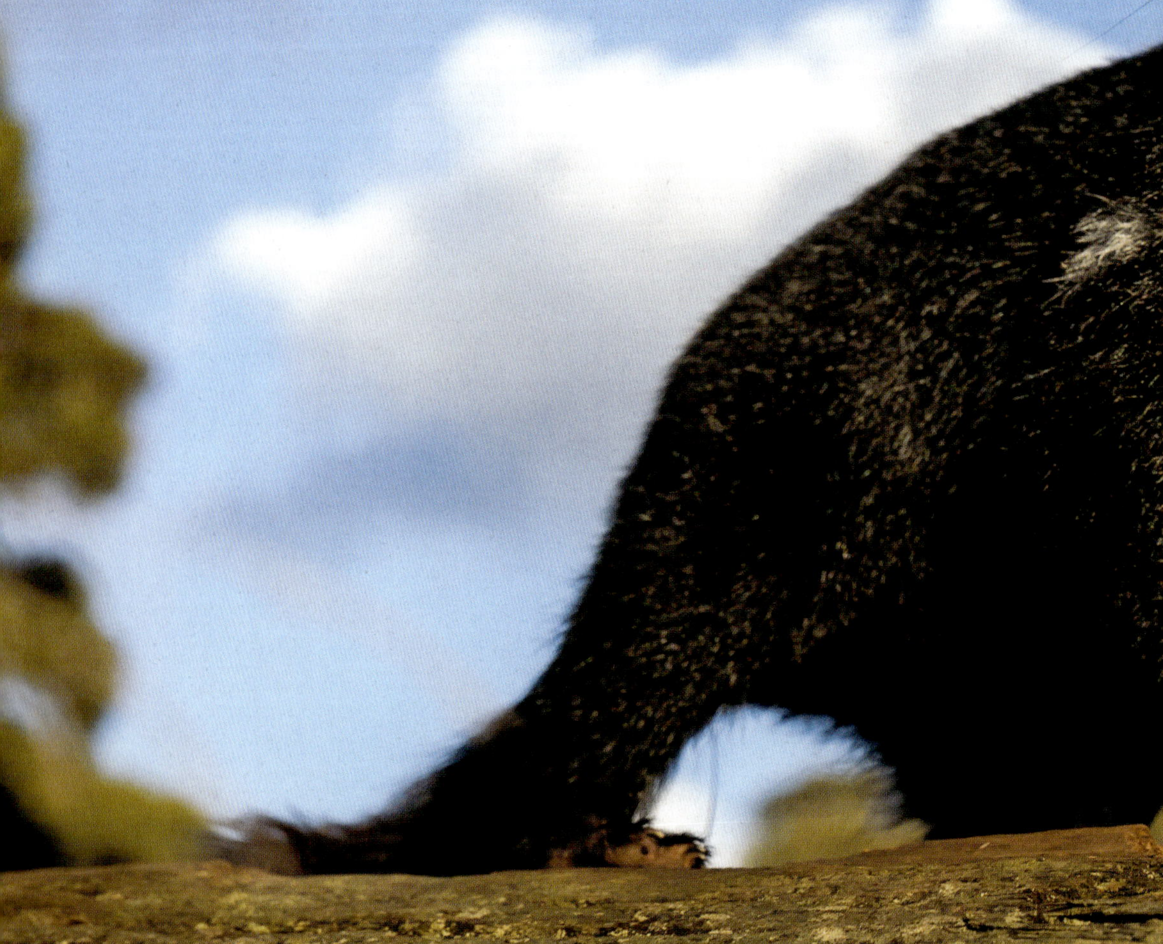

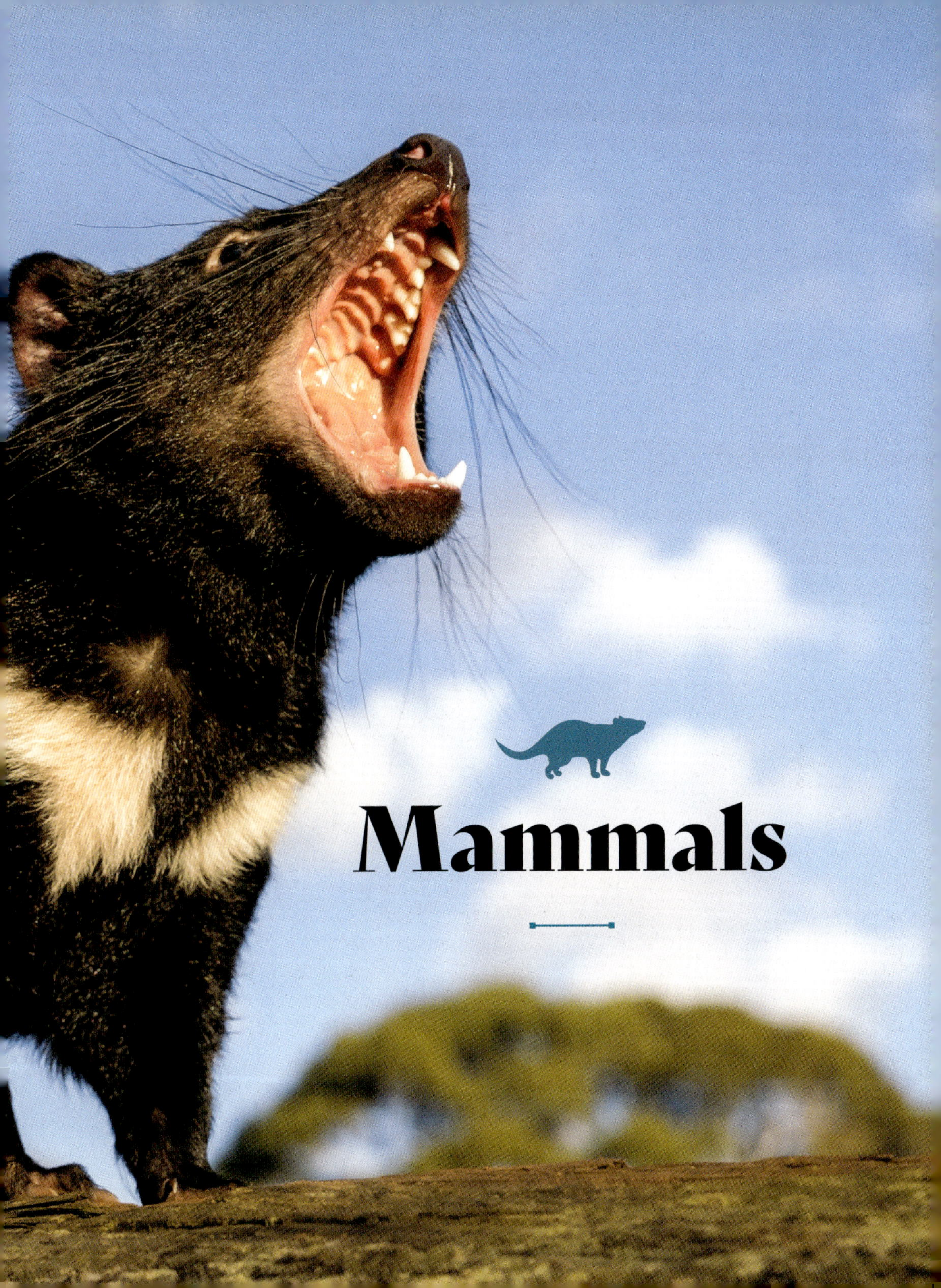

Mammals

Bilby

Macrotis lagotis

The bilby once occurred across 70 per cent of mainland Australia, but it is now listed as Vulnerable, and is disappearing rapidly. It's estimated that the population has fallen to less than 10,000, and today they can only be found in fragmented locations in Queensland, the Northern Territory and Western Australia. Sadly, their numbers have fallen significantly due to habitat loss and predation by feral cats and foxes.

Bilbies are known for their large, long ears and blue-grey fur. They are omnivores, eating a range of seeds, fungi, insects and small animals such as lizards. They dig extensively, helping with soil aeration and seed dispersal.

Words: Tim Faulkner.
Photograph: Robert McLean.

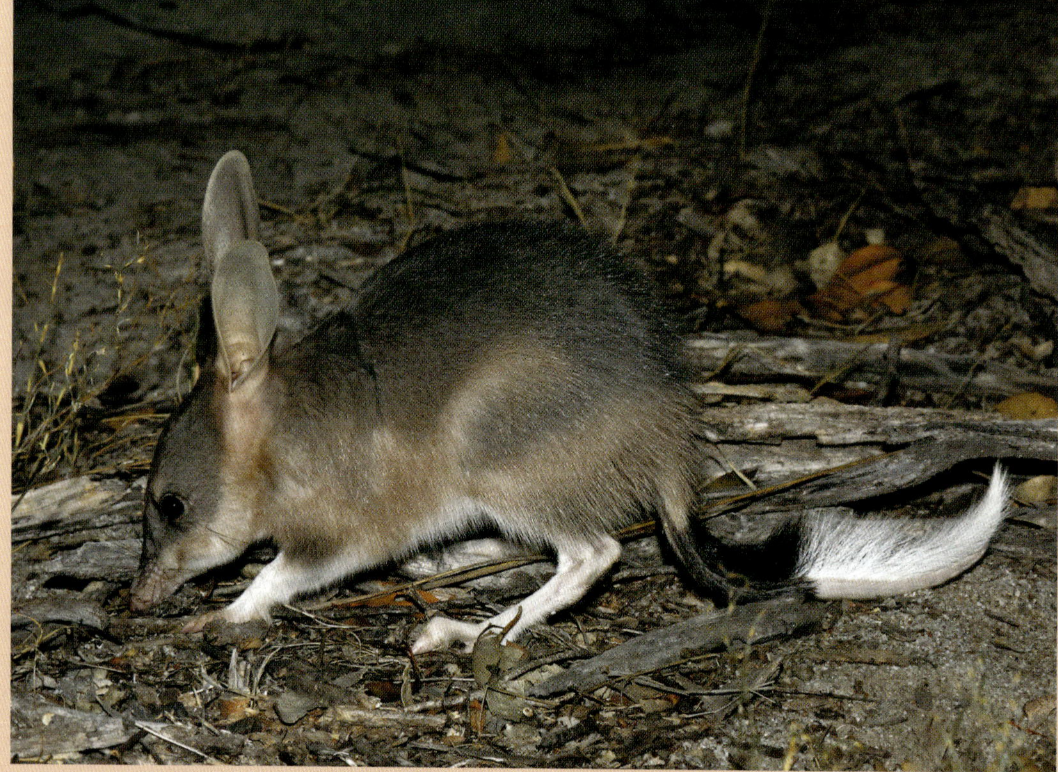

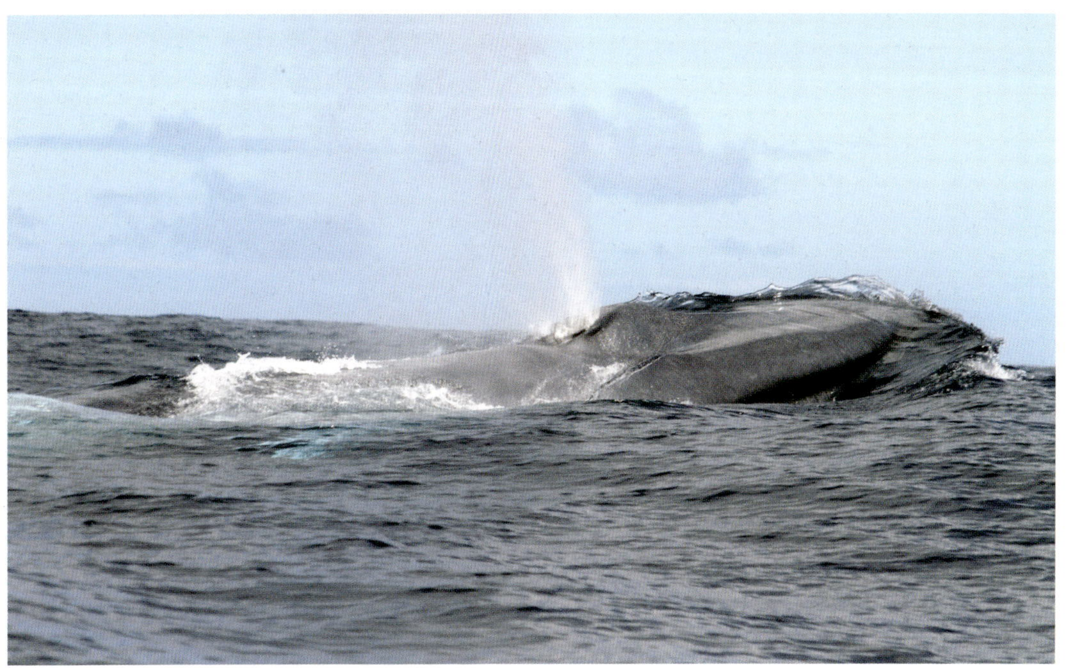

Blue Whale

Balaenoptera musculus, subspecies Pygmy Blue Whale *B. m. brevicauda*

The blue whale is the largest animal on the planet, and is an elusive species that most people have heard of but never seen. Twentieth century commercial whaling brought the blue whale close to the brink of extinction, and recovery is slow.

In Australian waters, it is mainly the pygmy blue whale subspecies that is found. And although they are called pygmy, they are only slightly shorter in size.

During the Australian summer months, when krill aggregates off southern and western Australia, pygmy blue whales travel to these waters to feed on the krill. Then they migrate north along the Western Australian coast to breed in warmer Indonesian waters, before migrating back to their feeding grounds.

Although commercial whaling is now banned, these cetaceans are exposed to a number of other threats, including ship strikes, underwater noise, and climate change – the latter impacting on krill, which they need in large amounts to survive.

Words and photograph:
Dr Kerstin Bilgmann.

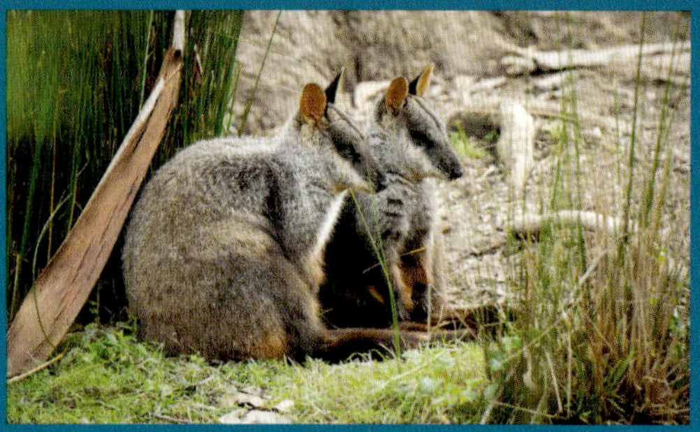

Brush-Tailed Rock-Wallaby

Petrogale penicillata

In Victoria, the brush-tailed rock-wallaby now exists in only two small and isolated locations, with less than 30 animals in each place. This agile species lives in rugged areas, and can bound great distances, up and across rocky terrain. They hide among the craggy ridges during the day, then emerge at dusk to feed on native grasses and other vegetation.

Brush-tailed rock-wallabies inhabit the region from south-eastern Queensland to eastern New South Wales and Victoria. They are recognised as three genetically distinct populations. The population known as the southern form is the one located in Victoria. Changes to habitat and the impact of feral cats, foxes and goats has caused the few remaining populations to become isolated. This separation has created a lack of genetic diversity within the populations, too – another significant threat to the survival of the species.

Words and photograph: Zoos Victoria.

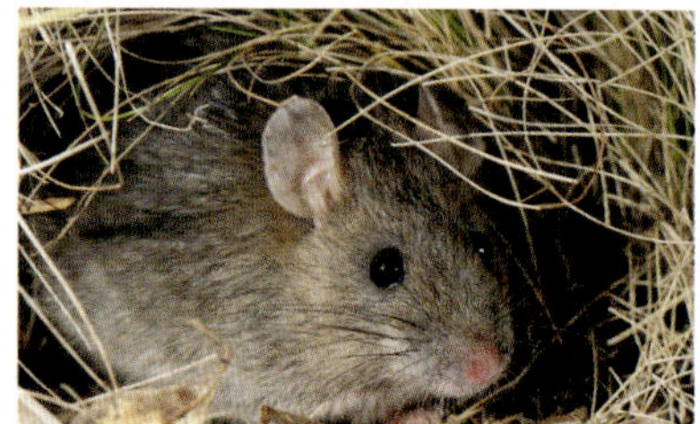

Hastings River Mouse

Pseudomys oralis

The Hastings River mouse is a rodent with a head-and-body length of about 17cm. It has brownish-grey fur above, buff to greyish-white fur below, and white feet. The 15cm-long tail is also furred white on the underside. It has large, bulging eyes surrounded by a black eye-ring, and a rounded snout.

Words and photograph: Saving Our Species.

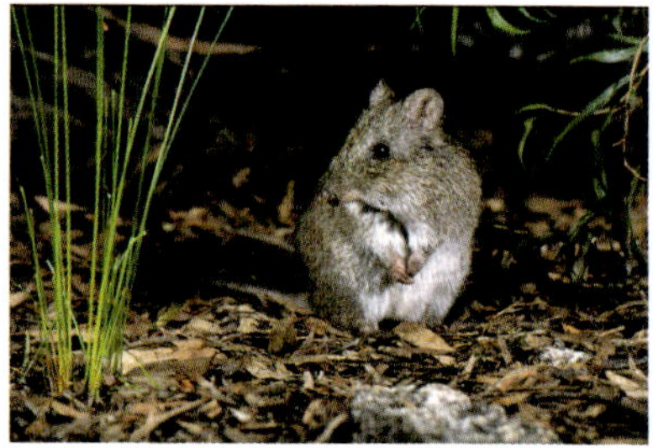

Gilbert's Potoroo

Potorous gilbertii

Gilbert's potoroo is a small kangaroo-like marsupial, slightly smaller than a rabbit, with a dense coat of soft grey-brown fur and a slender downwards curving snout. It is found only in a small area of the southern coast of Western Australia, and is thought to be Australia's rarest mammal, with only about 100 individuals known to be alive. It hadn't been recorded since the 1870s, and was believed to be extinct – until it was rediscovered on Mount Gardner at Two Peoples Bay in 1994. It is threatened by fire, predation by foxes and cats, lack of genetic diversity, and climate change.

Words: Gilbert's Potoroo Action Group.
Photograph: Dick Walker/GPAG.

Numbat

Myrmecobius fasciatus

The numbat was once widespread across southern and central Australia, but it is now extinct through most of its range, only surviving in small fragmented populations in Western Australia. Habitat loss, feral cats and foxes are causing the decline, and numbats are now endangered. It's estimated there are less than 1000 left in the wild.

Numbats have long bushy tails, and are reddish-brown on their shoulders and head, with the colour changing further down their body, to black with white stripes. They are an insectivore marsupial with an exclusive diet of termites, so they're also strictly diurnal – active during the day – which is unique, and associated with termite activity.

Words: Tim Faulkner.
Photograph: Robert McLean.

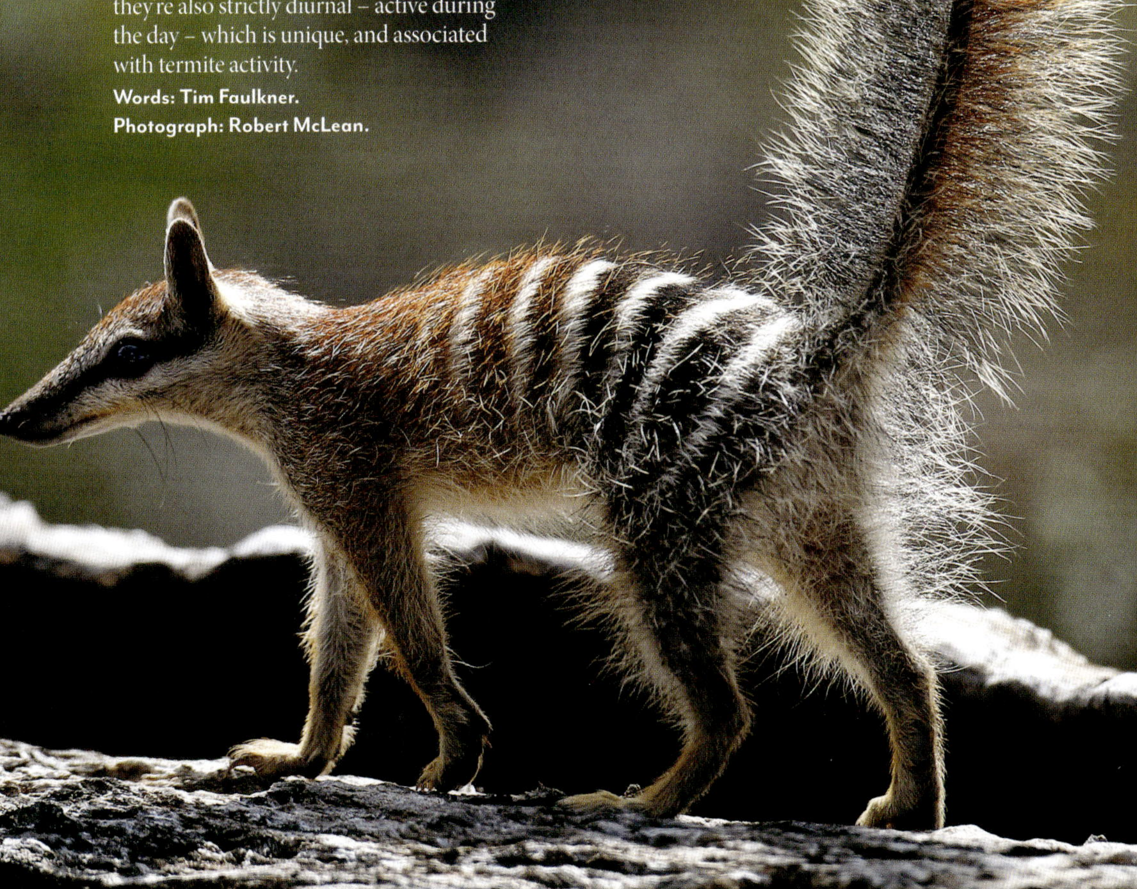

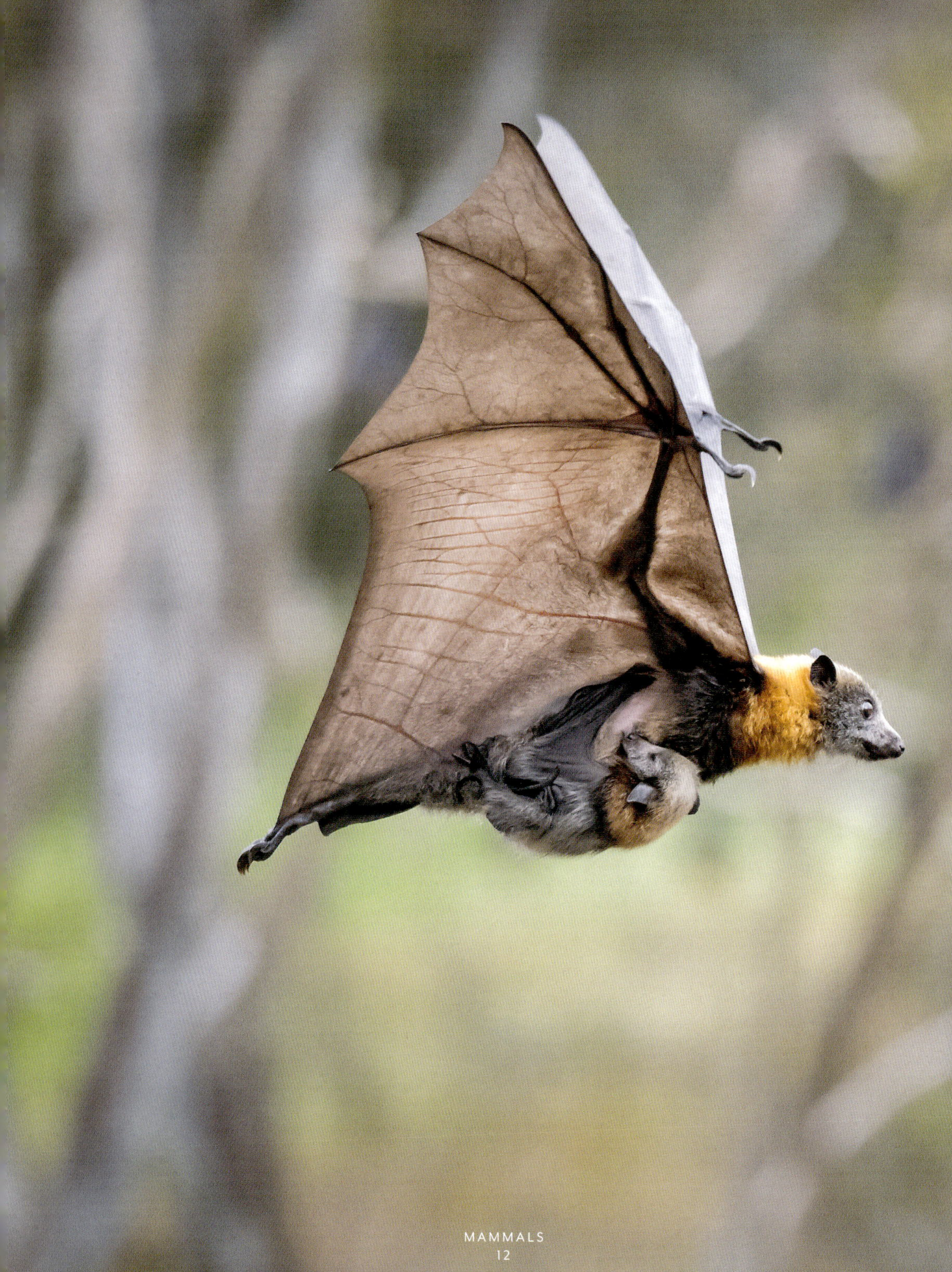

Grey-Headed Flying-Fox

Pteropus poliocephalus

As Australia's only endemic flying-fox, grey-headed flying-foxes have historically occupied the forests and woodlands of south-eastern Australia. As pollinators and seed dispersers, they are a vital keystone species, contributing to the reproductive and evolutionary processes of many forest communities.

Breeding only once a year, they normally give birth to just a single pup, and the pups stay attached to their mothers until they're too heavy to carry – at about four to five weeks of age.

Over the past 200 years, continued habitat destruction and the increasing frequency and severity of heat-stress events have reduced their population to a small fraction of what it once was. They are now listed as Vulnerable to extinction.

Words and photograph: Doug Gimesy.

Southern Bent-Wing Bat

Miniopterus orianae bassanii

Once numbering in the hundreds of thousands, the southern bent-wing bat has declined dramatically in recent decades, and is now listed as Critically Endangered.

This bat is confined to south-eastern South Australia and south-western Victoria, where it roosts exclusively in caves. Over summer its roosting requirements are specific, with females congregating to breed in just three maternity caves. Females give birth to one pup a year and invest heavily in maternal care, with the young suckling on her rich milk until it is the same size as its mother. At night the adults fly large distances (70km or more) to forage, feeding largely on moths, including agricultural pests, typically consuming half their body weight in insects in a night.

Words : Zoos Victoria.
Photograph: Lindy Lumsden.

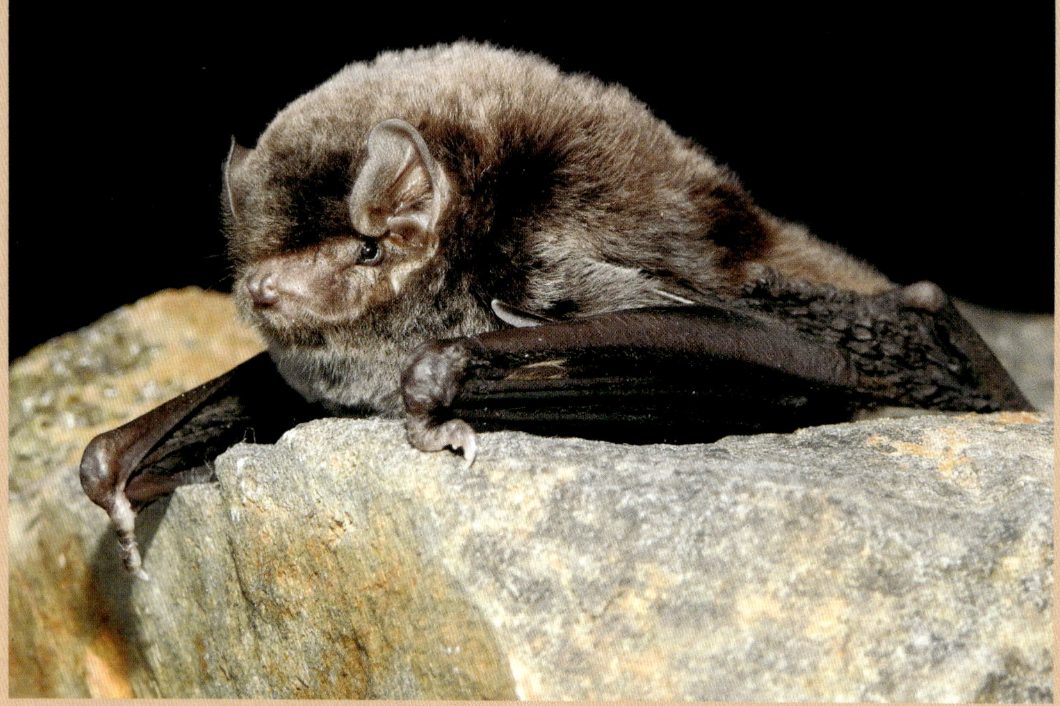

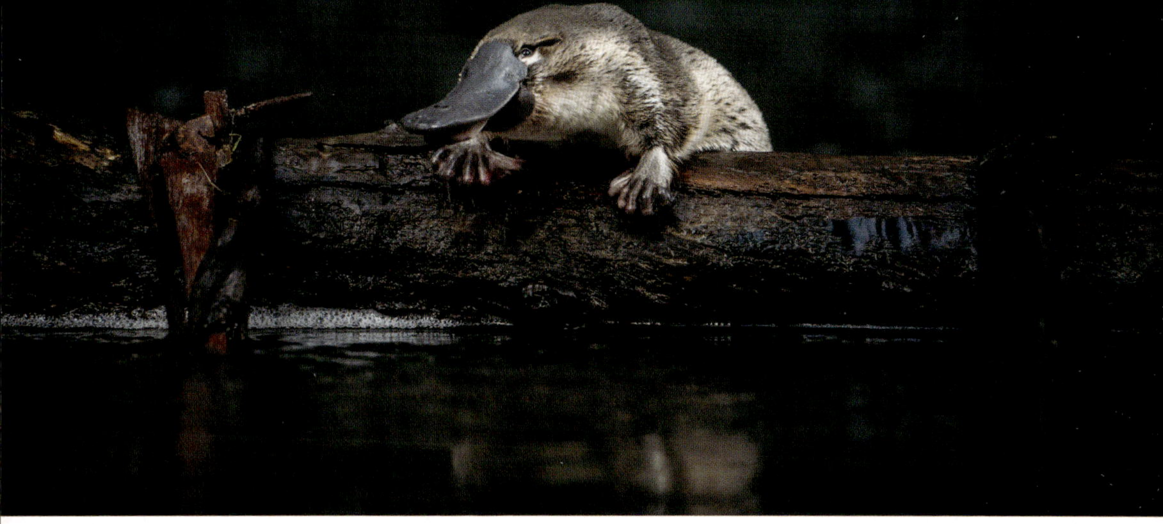

Platypus

Ornithorhynchus anatinus

Found in freshwater systems along the east coast of Australia as well as in Tasmania, platypuses are one of the top predators found in the waterways they live in, helping maintain ecosystem balance and health.

One of only two Australian egg-laying mammals – the other being the echidna – the platypus is truly amazing. The adults have no teeth, so grind their food with hard keratin pads; the young drink their mother's milk by licking it off her skin, and the males have venomous spurs on their back ankles – making them one of only a few venomous mammals in the world. Platypuses swim with their eyes closed, finding their way and searching for food using pressure and electrical sensors in their bills – a kind of sixth sense.

However, human-driven impacts from activities like land clearing and dam building, as well as bushfires and droughts, continue to destroy their habitats. In the past 30 years, platypuses have disappeared from more than 20 per cent of the waterways they once called home.

Words and photograph: Doug Gimesy.

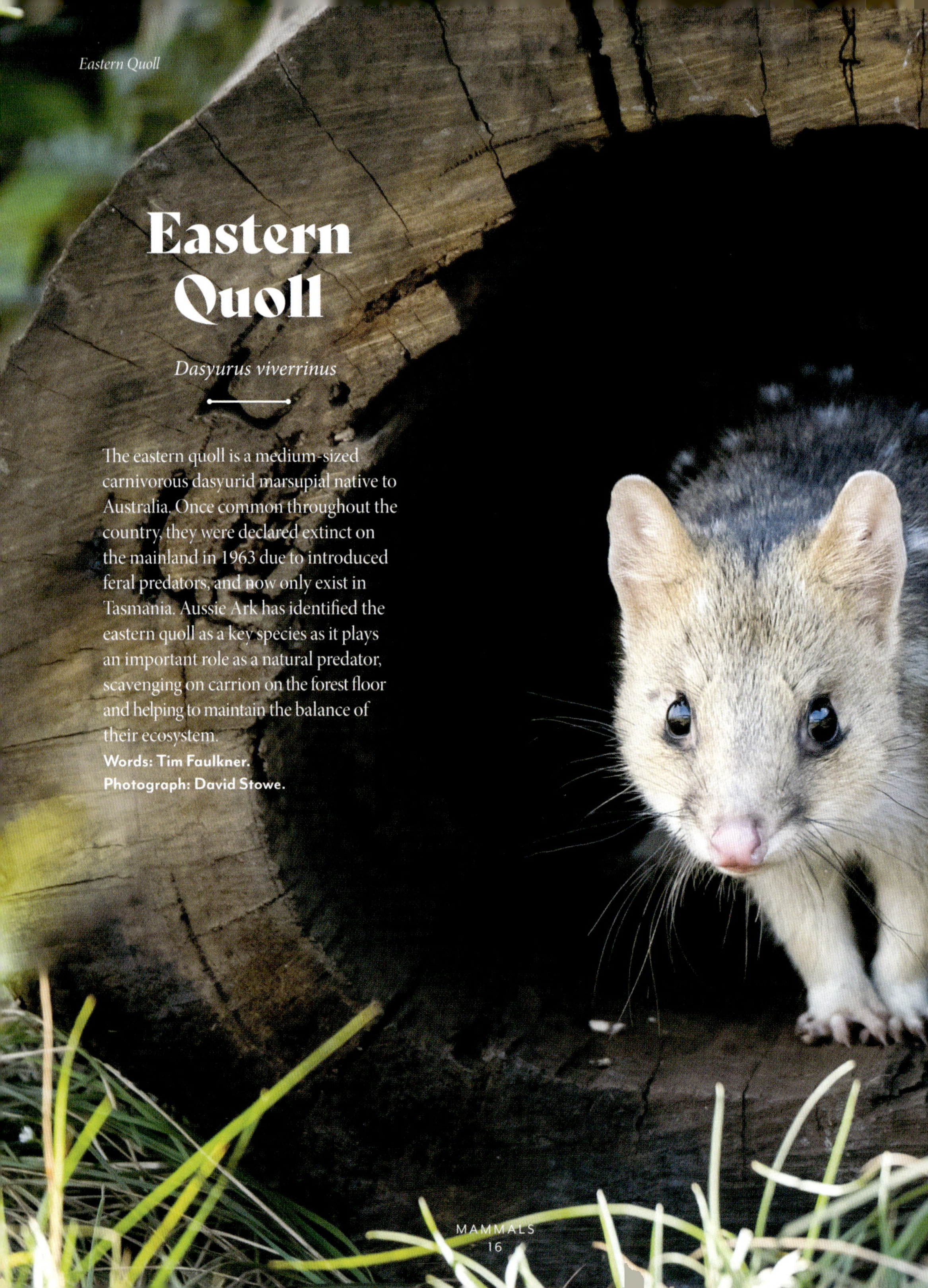

Eastern Quoll

Dasyurus viverrinus

The eastern quoll is a medium-sized carnivorous dasyurid marsupial native to Australia. Once common throughout the country, they were declared extinct on the mainland in 1963 due to introduced feral predators, and now only exist in Tasmania. Aussie Ark has identified the eastern quoll as a key species as it plays an important role as a natural predator, scavenging on carrion on the forest floor and helping to maintain the balance of their ecosystem.

Words: Tim Faulkner.
Photograph: David Stowe.

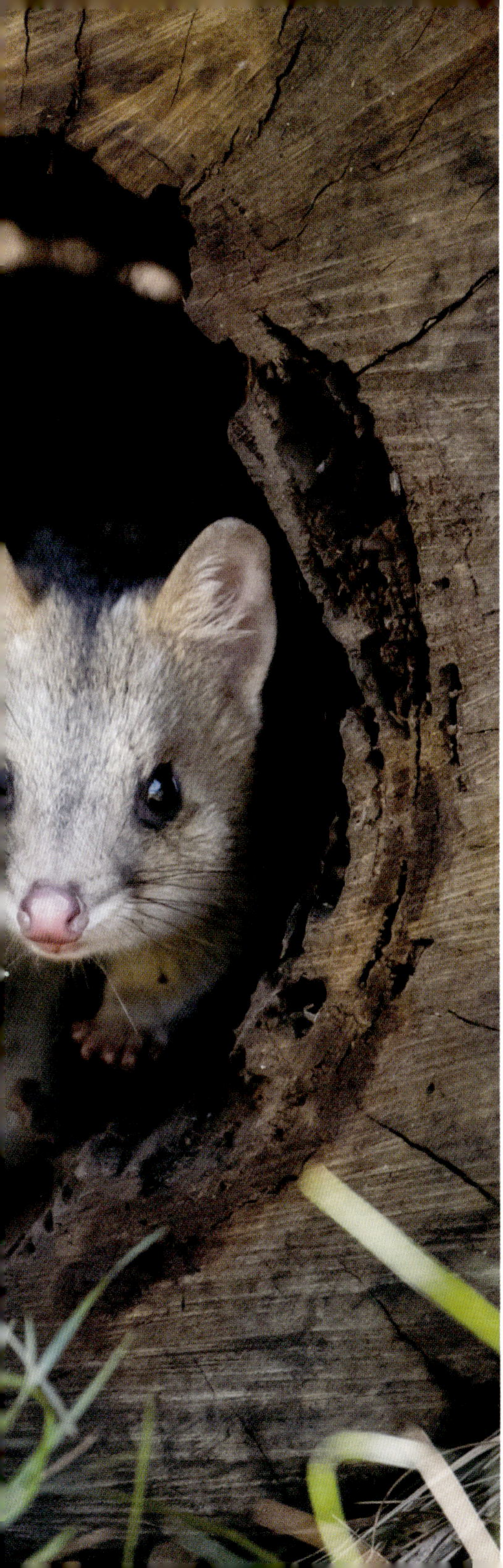

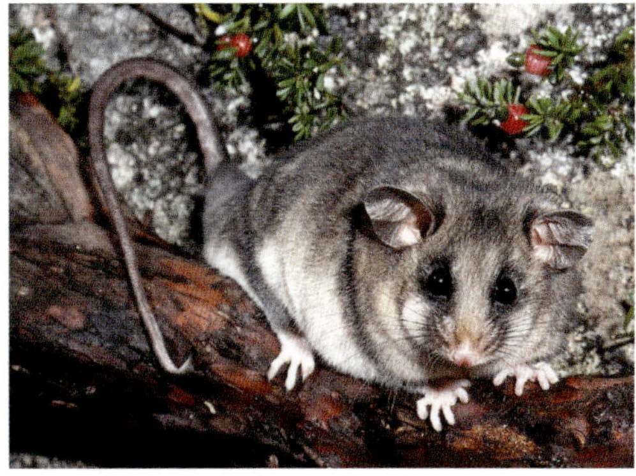

Mountain Pygmy-Possum

Burramys parvus

The mountain pygmy-possum lives only in alpine and subalpine areas on the highest mountains of Victoria and New South Wales. In NSW, the entire range is in a 30km by 8km area of Kosciuszko National Park between Thredbo and Kerries Ridge, where it occupies less than 4km^2 of habitat. This small marsupial spends spring and summer fattening up on bogong moths and the fruit of the mountain plum-pine, before spending winter in torpor underneath a blanket of thick snow.

Words and photograph: SoS.

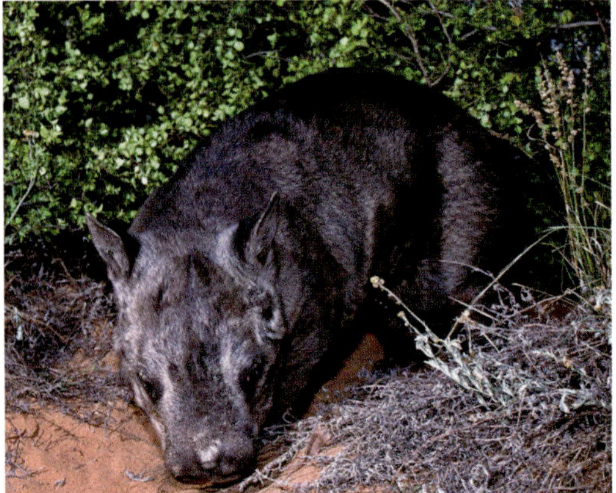

Northern Hairy-Nosed Wombat

Lasiorhinus krefftii

The northern hairy-nosed wombat is one of the rarest land mammals in the world, and is Critically Endangered. It was once found from Queensland through NSW and south to the Victorian border, but it's now found only in one place – Epping Forest National Park in central Queensland. It's estimated there are only about 300 individuals remaining. These wombats have suffered from land clearing for agricultural grazing, and were directly persecuted as a pest. Their survival is a direct result of ongoing conservation management.

Words: Tim Faulkner.
Photograph: Queensland Government.

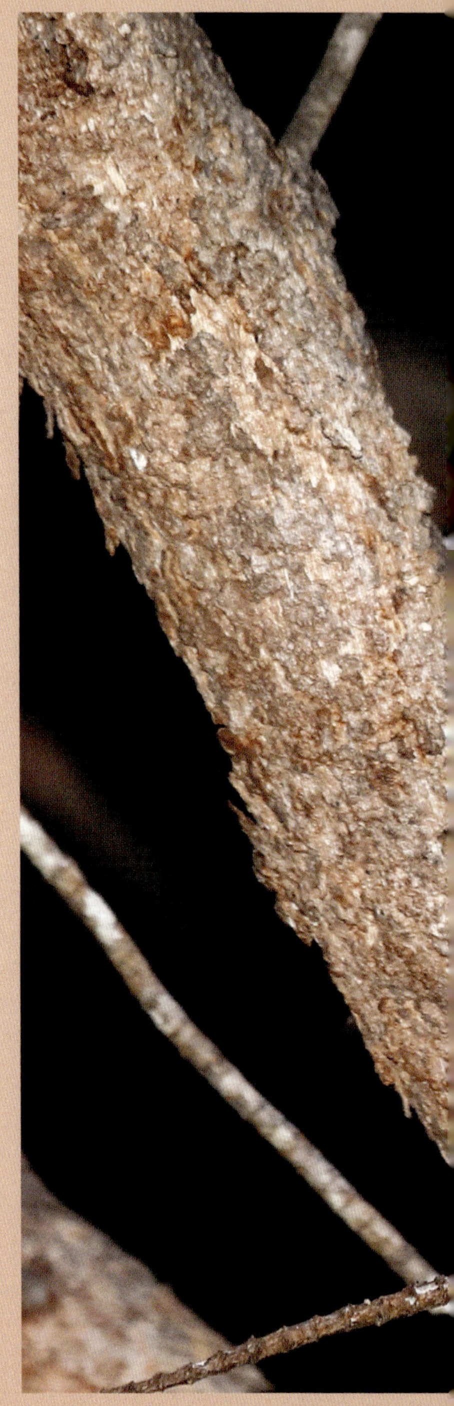

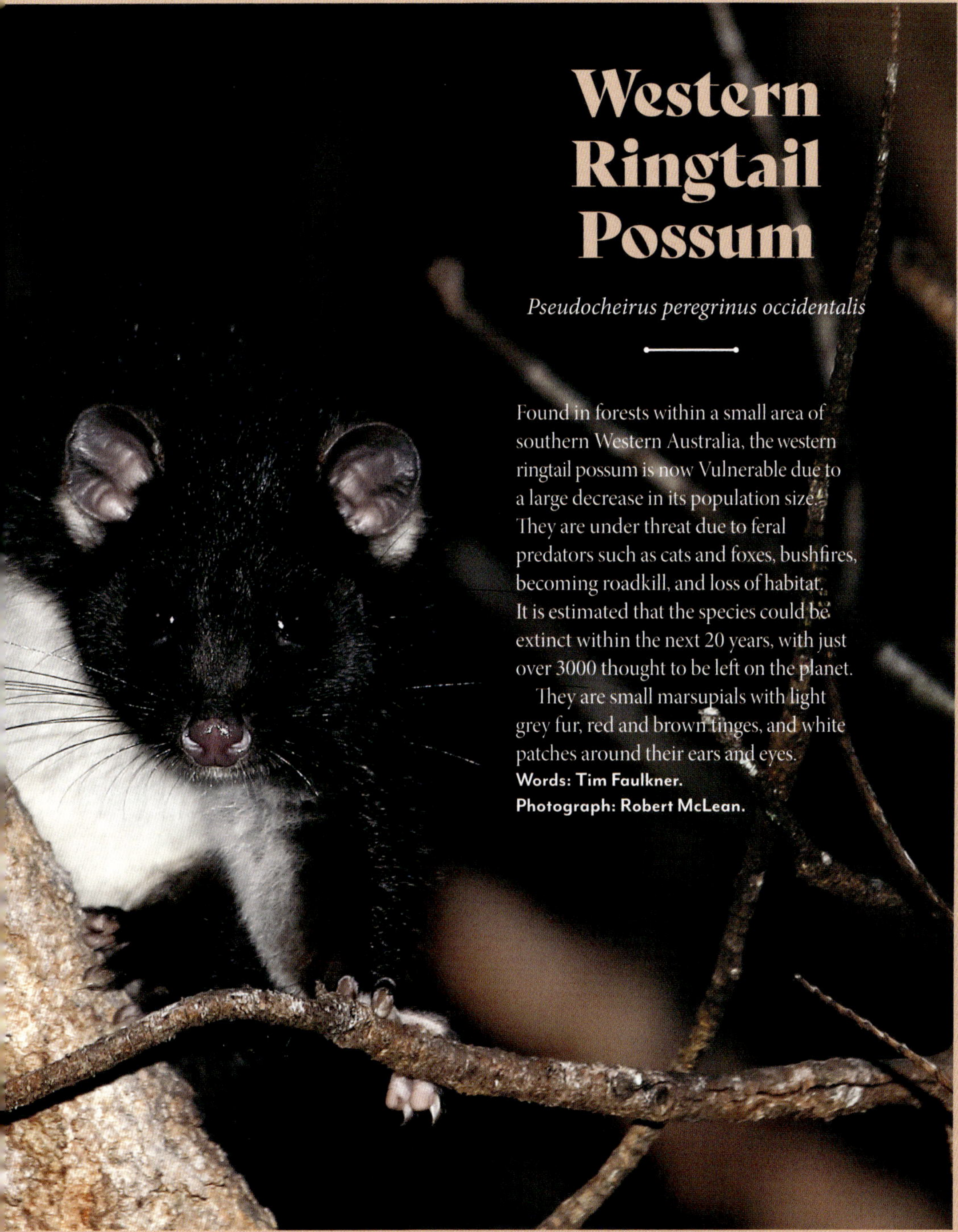

Western Ringtail Possum

Pseudocheirus peregrinus occidentalis

Found in forests within a small area of southern Western Australia, the western ringtail possum is now Vulnerable due to a large decrease in its population size. They are under threat due to feral predators such as cats and foxes, bushfires, becoming roadkill, and loss of habitat. It is estimated that the species could be extinct within the next 20 years, with just over 3000 thought to be left on the planet.

They are small marsupials with light grey fur, red and brown tinges, and white patches around their ears and eyes.

Words: Tim Faulkner.
Photograph: Robert McLean.

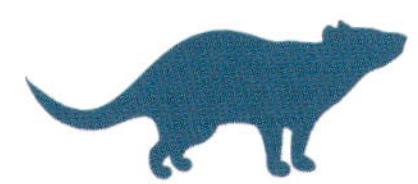

Tim Faulkner

Aussie Ark founder

Our geographic isolation has allowed us to become one of the most important places on earth for biodiversity. Much of our wildlife is found nowhere else, making its conservation even more critical – a whopping 87 per cent of our mammals, 93 per cent of our reptiles, 94 per cent of our frogs, and 45 per cent of our birds are only found in Australia.

Yet Australia has the second-highest rate of overall biodiversity loss, next to Indonesia, in the world. As of 2021, more than 1700 species of plants, animals and ecological communities are at risk of extinction. We have the worst extinction rate on earth, and have lost more mammal and plant species than any other country in the past 200 years.

Today, one in three of our native mammals are at *imminent* risk of extinction. In March 2021 alone, another 13 species were added to the extinct species list, but the actual number will be much higher, as species aren't listed as extinct until a period of 50 years passes without them being seen. Which means that right now that number is much higher, simply because species have not yet met that sad criteria.

We have the worst extinction rate on earth, and have lost more mammal and plant species than any other country in the past 200 years.

We are fighting this battle on all fronts. Deforestation continues, despite nearly half of all our forests already being lost. Critical habitat is being swallowed up by developments, turned into farmland or lost to climate change in drought or flood.

The biggest single threat to our wildlife right now though is feral animals. They are literally eating our endangered species alive. The feral pest invasion is as real as it is unfathomable, species such as the feral cat, fox, pig, horse, rat, mouse, goat, rabbit,

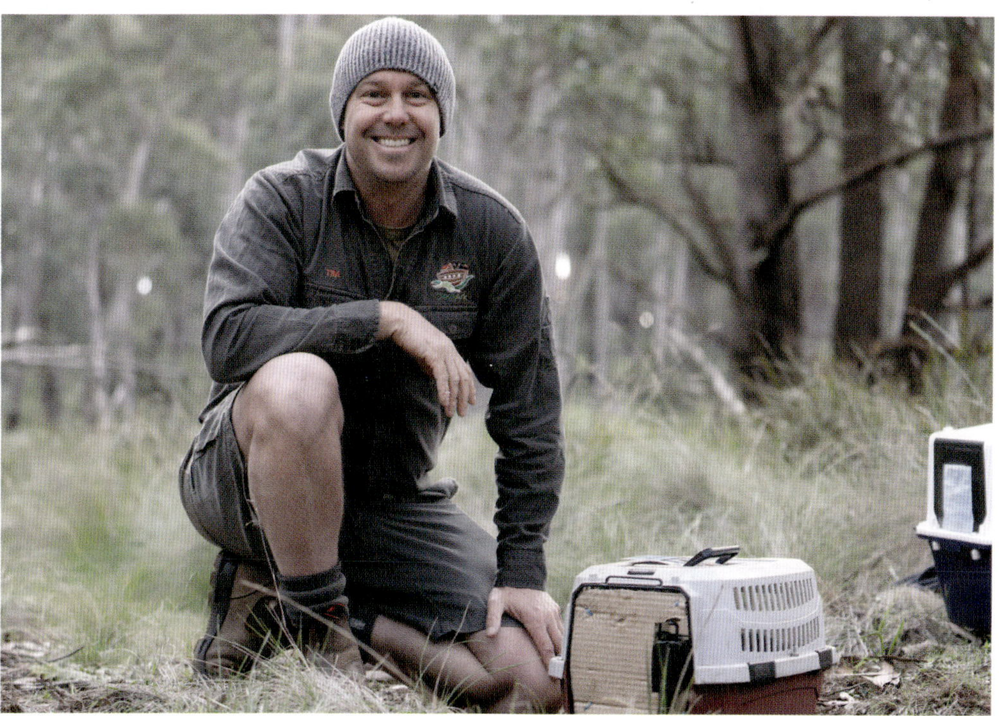

deer, buffalo and camel are taking over and wreaking havoc. Our native species have never encountered such fierce predation, or undergone the evolution needed to counter it.

There is hope though, and we can turn this situation around, but it isn't going to be an easy ride. We need a rapid upscaling of feral pest control, especially within our national parks. Additionally, we need more feral-free fenced sanctuaries, like those found at Aussie Ark, to provide safe havens for our threatened natives.

Our environmental laws also need a radical overhaul to stop us from operating within an endless loop of 'risk assess' and 'risk mitigate' – it's getting us nowhere. The Australian Government has to step up to the plate and engage in both public and private business relationships to affect real change. Universities need to change tack and utilise applied science rather than the traditional research model.

Lastly, and I think most importantly, we need to help our kids be the future. We need to get them out in the bush and invested in our habitat and species. We can teach them the skills, but we need to develop their character and passion to see it through to the very end. The only way we will get through this is together.

Photograph: Aussie Ark.

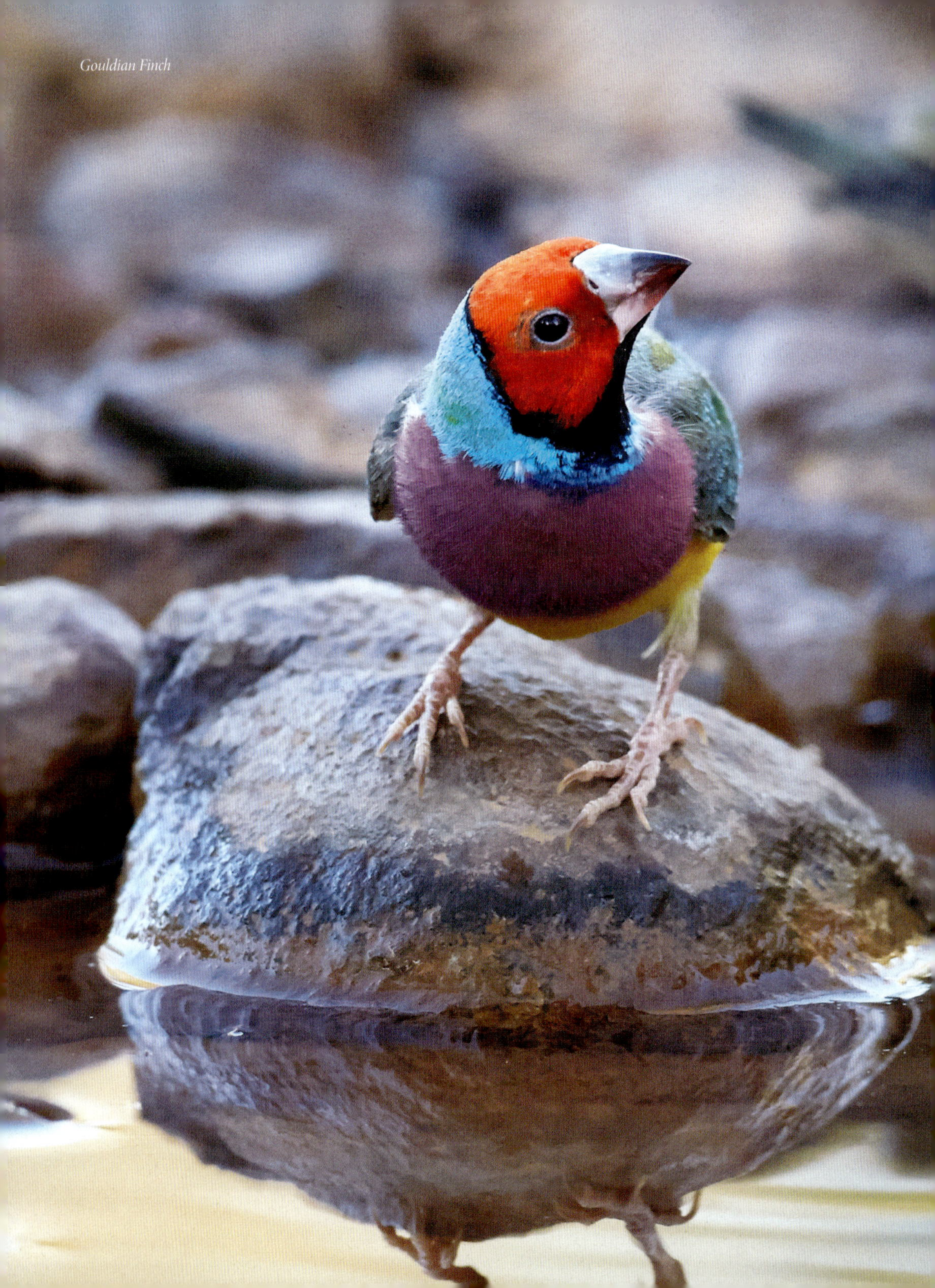
Gouldian Finch

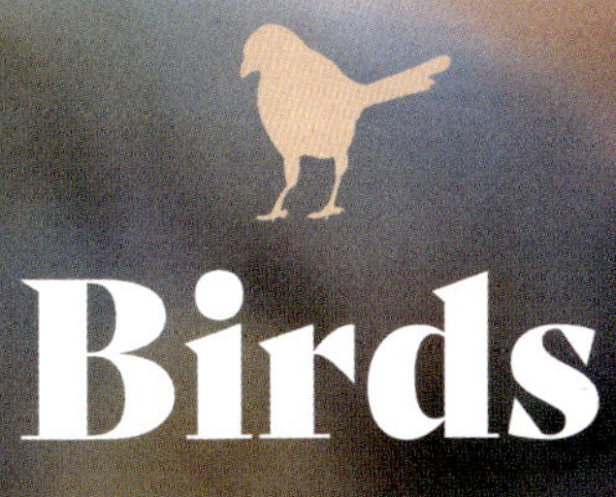

Birds

Gouldian Finch

Erythrura gouldiae

The Gouldian finch is often regarded as one of the most beautiful small songbirds in the world. It comes in two morphs – the red head and the black head.

Up until the early 1980s, large numbers were trapped in the wild for the local and international bird trade. However, the Gouldian finch's decline has been caused by habitat changes due to land clearing and fire management.

Fire plays a large role in their survival. In the dry season, they rely on controlled fires to burn the undergrowth, so they can feed on seeds on the ground. In the wet season, they like to live in areas which have been burned in the previous dry season. This produces lush new growth with plenty of seeds to eat.

Budgerigars, sulphur-crested cockatoos and finches are ambassadors for Australia worldwide. Australian finches, especially zebra finches and Gouldian finches, adorn many households as pets, are studied in laboratories, and are far more numerous in captivity than they are now in their home country in the wild.

Words: Prof. Gisela Kaplan.
Photograph: Martin Wallis/AWC.

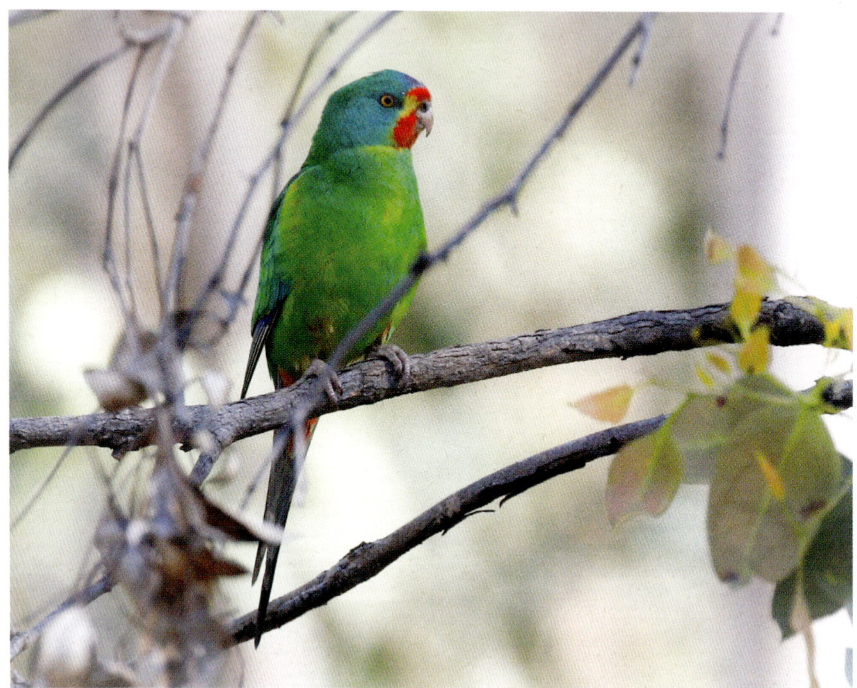

Swift Parrot

Lathamus discolour

A small parrot, rightly called 'swift' because it flies very fast (it's been clocked at 88km/h!). Swift parrots are nomadic migrants, living on nectar and lerps (sweet secretion by lice living on eucalypt trees), and going where the food is. They still occur throughout much of Australia, except Western Australia and the Northern Territory. They breed in Tasmania, arriving there between August and October, co-timed with the flowering of the Tasmanian blue gum, then migrate to the mainland in autumn.

It has been known since the 1990s that native hollow-bearing trees are indispensable for as many as 270 Australian species, especially for native parrots and cockatoos. Yet these habitat tress have continued to be cut down, leading to a sharp decline in birds. Over the past 20 years alone, about 23 per cent of the swift parrots' breeding habitat in Tasmania's southern forests has disappeared, leading to greater competition and predation by sugar gliders.

It is only by strong support via recovery plans and many volunteers that this bird is still around.

Words: Prof. Gisela Kaplan. Photograph: Mick Roderick courtesy Mindaribba LALC.

Orange-Bellied Parrot

Neophema chrysogaster

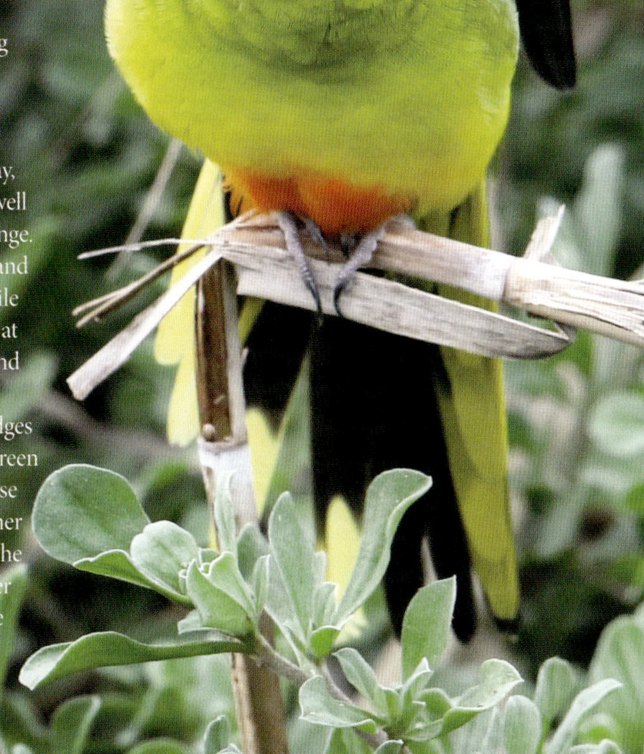

The orange-bellied parrot is one of just three parrot species worldwide that migrates seasonally. The species overwinters in the southern coastal areas of Victoria and South Australia, but returns to Tasmania to breed, with the only active breeding sites being in the remote south-western region of Melaleuca.

Degradation of wintering quarters and changes to fire management are thought to be contributing to their decline. Hence rehabilitating the southern mainland coastal wetlands (including mangrove forests, saltmarshes and seagrass meadows), which is now underway, is vital for the parrots' survival as well as in the fight against climate change. For the parrots, some scrubland and marshes can be food sources, while intact wetlands sequester carbon at a much higher rate than forests and grasslands.

Note the beautiful dark blue edges of the flight feathers against the green and yellow body, and the turquoise ridge over the nares. This is another indigenous parrot exemplifying the plight of parrots worldwide – over a third of all psittacine species are now endangered.

Words: Prof. Gisela Kaplan.
Photograph: Andrew Silcocks.

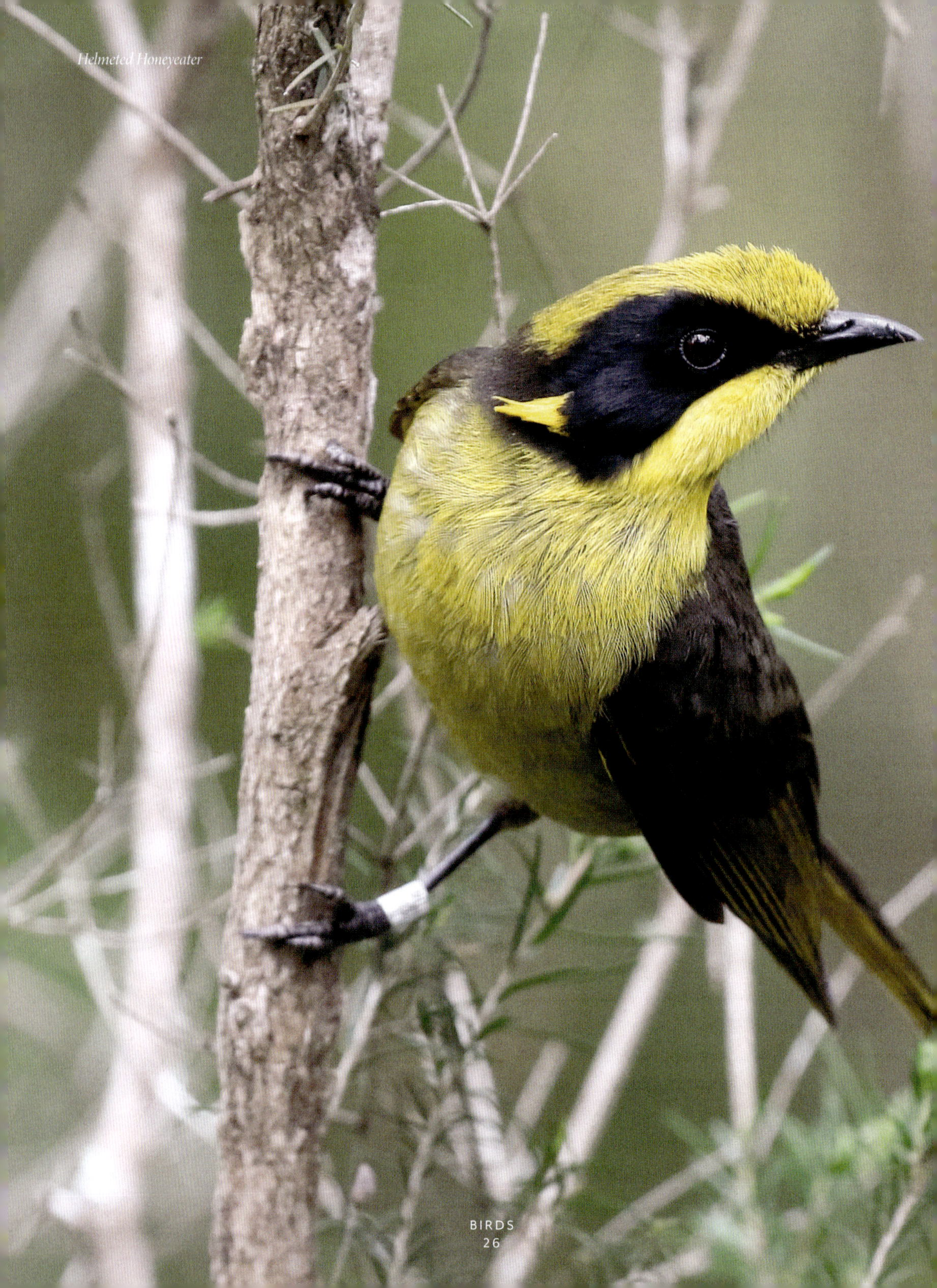

Helmeted Honeyeater

Helmeted Honeyeater

Lichenostomus melanops cassidix

The helmeted honeyeater is dramatic in its sharply delineated black and bright yellow plumage, and it gets its name from the golden plush-like forehead feathers that resemble a helmet.

In 1989, it was discovered that this subspecies of the yellow-tufted honeyeater, endemic to Victoria, was down to 50 birds, and confined to a small strip of the Yellingbo Nature Conservation Reserve east of Melbourne. Around this time, the Friends of the Helmeted Honeyeater was formed.

Its decline came as a surprise as this feisty little songbird has all the abilities to be flexible and survive. They are intolerant of other species and know how to defend themselves, and are territorial and nearly omnivorous, although preferring nectar, manna and lerp. Their extended breeding season of July to March, long even by Australian standards, is also in their favour.

But there is a problem: the dense riparian vegetation along riverbanks, which they prefer, has experienced die-off of its mountain swamp gum community, with little regeneration. Furthermore, degrading forest environments, whether near rivers or deep in forests, bring in assertive bell miners that evict other species. Despite substantial efforts, the future of this bird is still uncertain.

Words: Prof. Gisela Kaplan.
Photograph: Andrew Silcocks.

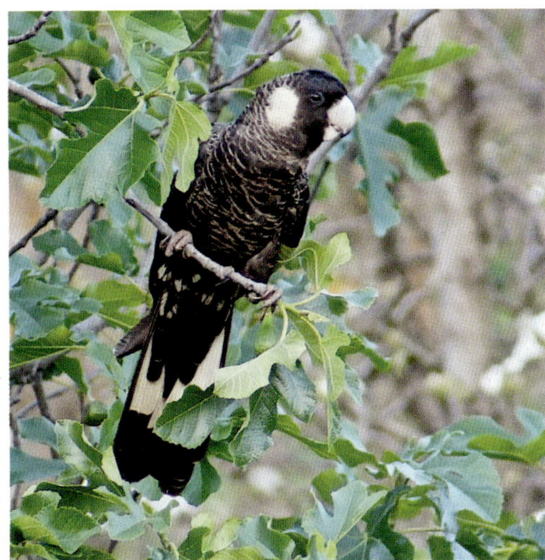

Carnaby's Black Cockatoo

Calyptorhynchus latirostris

This short-billed black cockatoo is iconic in Western Australia, and is now found only in the state's south and south-west. Males and females look alike, but they can be distinguished by the colour of their eye rings (pink in males, grey in females). All cockatoos use their feet like a hand for feeding, holding seed cones like ice-creams.

The problem with long-lived birds is that old birds are around for a long time, masking the problem when there are, in fact, not many young to follow. Each bird returns to the same nest site each year. The pair generally stays together for life, and the removal of nesting trees leaves them unable to breed. Suitable natural nest holes for such large-sized birds can take 150 years of tree growth to develop.

Around 87 per cent of the Carnaby's black cockatoo habitat in WA's Wheatbelt has been cleared, where thousands used to flock.

Words: Prof. Gisela Kaplan.
Photograph: Bobbi Marchini.

Regent Honeyeater

Anthochaera Phrygia

The regent honeyeater has icon status in NSW. It is the rarest songbird in Australia's temperate forests, a great mimic, and very important for the ecosystem. With their brilliant flashes of yellow, they could once be seen in their hundreds. As a flocking species, breeding success partly depends on numbers to defend their plot and their young, but numbers are now very low (about 300).

Regent honeyeaters are nomads, flying quickly from one abundant nectar patch to another, thus acting as important pollinators for flowering trees. They also feed on other plant sugars, as well as on insects, spiders, and mistletoe. Widespread clearance of their woodland habitat, and competition for nectar from larger, more aggressive honeyeaters, have contributed to their dramatic decline over the past 30 years.

Today, they are now largely confined to the periphery of the Greater Blue Mountains, but active recovery plans may yet lead to an increase in numbers.

Words: Prof. Gisela Kaplan.
Photograph: Mick Roderick.

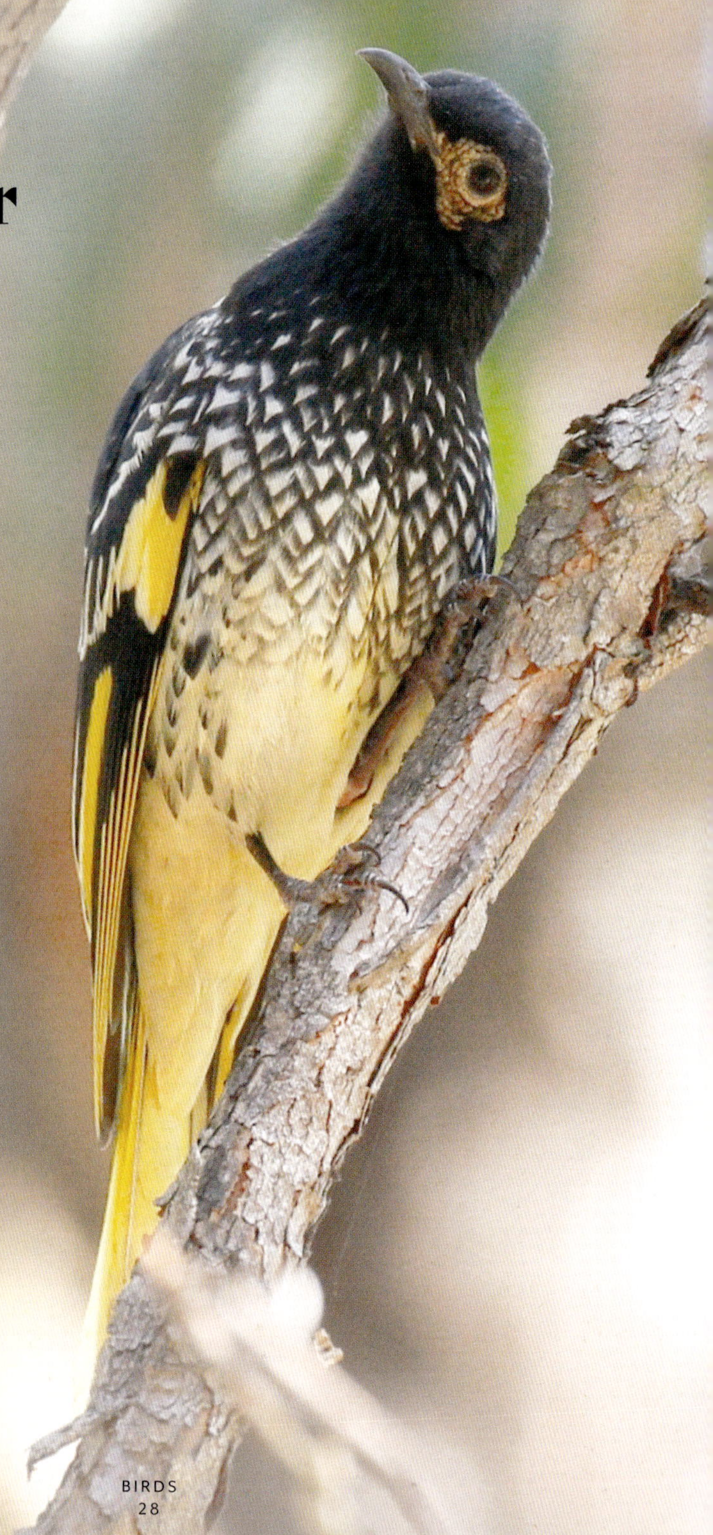

Forty-Spotted Pardalote

Pardalotus quadragintus

This tiny songbird (just 9-10cm) is very energetic, and is the rarest in the family of pardalotes. Bruny Island and Maria Island off Tasmania are now the only refuges for this species. The bird feeds on white gum, *Eucalyptus viminalis*, and while nestlings are largely fed on its manna, they're also active insect hunters. Unusually, they may choose tree hollows or ground burrows as nest sites.

Studies show a decline of 47 per cent between 1991 and 1997 alone. Apart from the typical range of problems that have caused the decline of avian species, including habitat loss, this species has a problem with a parasite, a screw worm fly, *Passeromyia longicornis*, which lays its eggs in their nests. The resulting maggots then burrow into the skin of the nestlings and feed on their blood, contributing to their very high mortality rate.

Words: Prof. Gisela Kaplan.
Photograph: Lachlan Story.

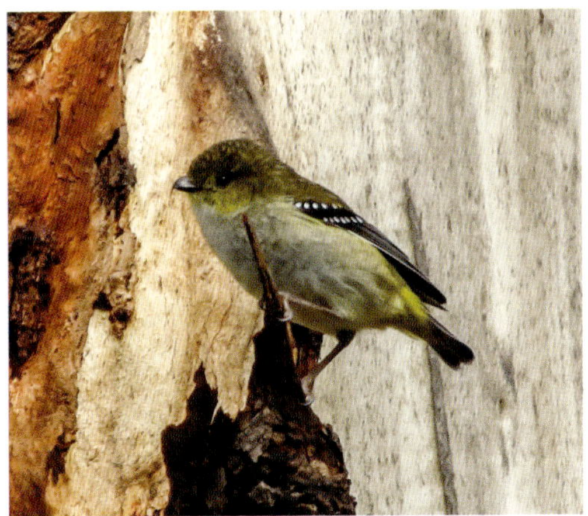

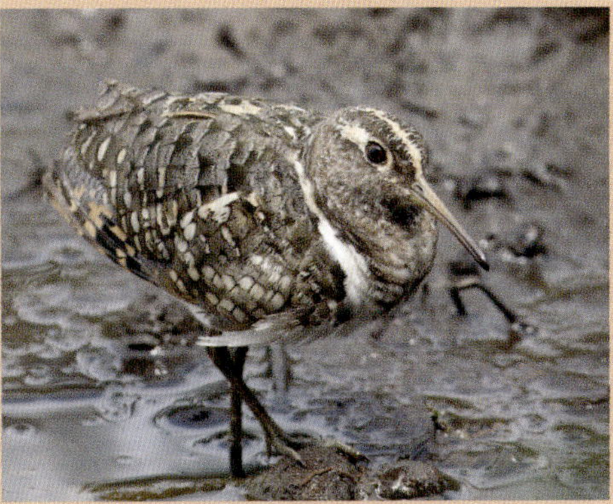

Australian Painted Snipe

Rostratula australis

This beautifully patterned bird is quite enigmatic, especially as it forages at night – and, at any time of day, it freezes and stands motionless if it detects any disturbance.

Snipes often walk together in small bands of males, and prefer slushy, muddy, water-drenched grounds. They find crustaceans, worms, snails and other items by probing with their beak. Note the very large, high-set eyes – they offer low-range binocular vision while the bird eats, and also helps the bird keep watch overhead for potential predators.

As is the case with bitterns, the painted snipe's status as Endangered is directly attributable to human activity, as wetlands are drained and water is diverted from major rivers for irrigation. This means that shallow wetlands cannot form in natural overflow areas. As a result, an entire ecosystem that's highly important for correcting water movement, filtering water, and keeping the land healthy, is destroyed. Birds like this rare snipe are indicators of the health of the ecosystem.

Words: Prof. Gisela Kaplan.
Photograph: Andrew Silcocks.

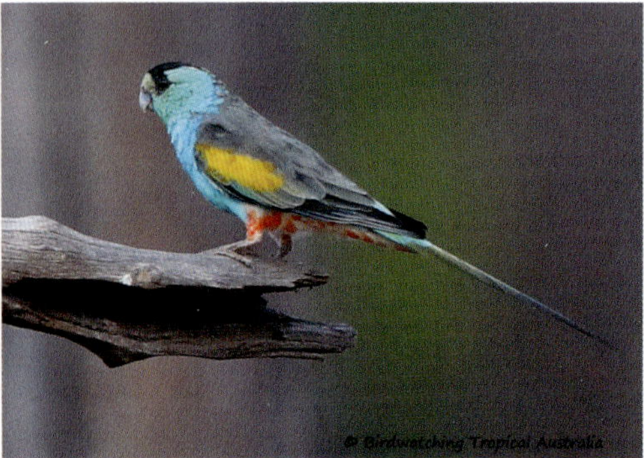

Golden-Shouldered Parrot

Burramys parvus

The golden-shouldered parrot is a highly treasured bird of the Cape York Peninsula. Males and females differ in appearance. The image above shows a male – it has a turquoise front, a salmon-coloured lower belly, and a black ridge above its beak that isn't present in the female (plus her belly is green and buff).

Remarkably, this species requires termite mounds for breeding, and digs tunnels into them that end in a nesting chamber. Many of these nest chambers remain entirely clean despite four or more nestlings occupying it, because of a symbiotic relationship with moth larvae, which feed on their faeces.

The golden-shouldered parrot feeds entirely on seeds of small grass species and, seasonally, almost exclusively on firegrass, *Schizachyrium fragile*. This has put them in a Vulnerable position because such grasses can be burnt, eaten by cattle or drowned by excessive rainfall. Also, pigs dig out nests and nestlings, and feral cats are also a constant risk.

Over the years, attempts have been made to improve the position of these parrots – and it seems that these efforts have, at least, stabilised their population.

Words: Prof. Gisela Kaplan.
Photograph: Doug Herrington.

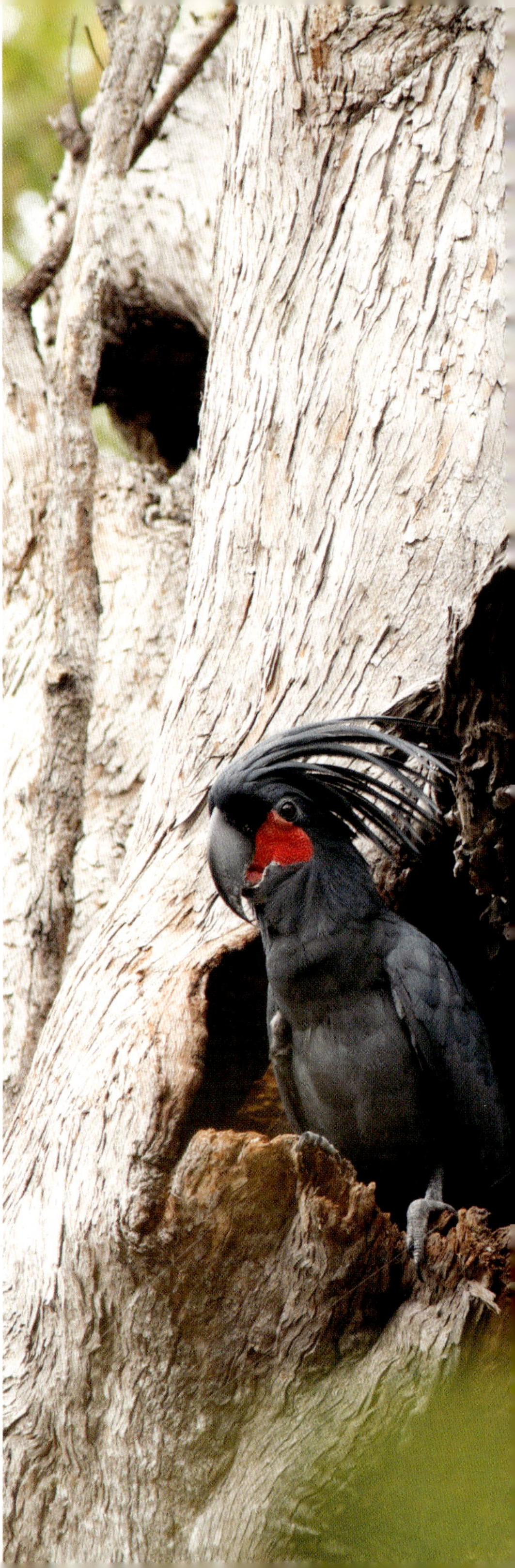

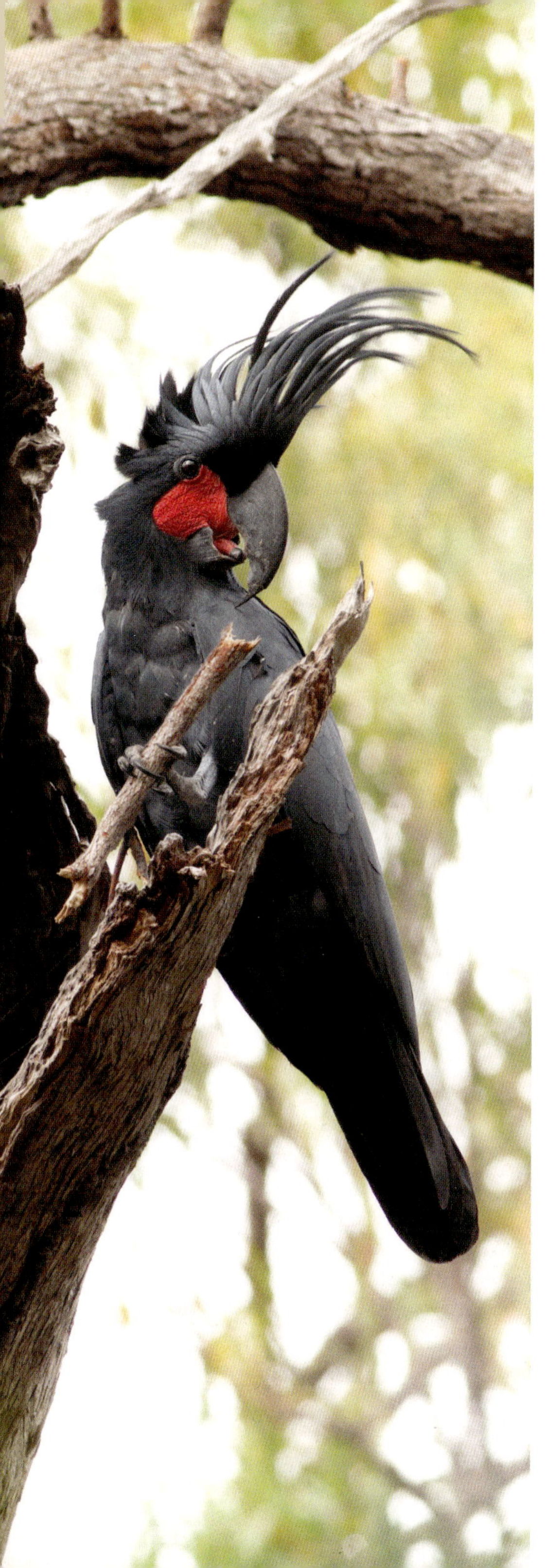

Palm Cockatoo

Probosciger aterrimus

Palm cockatoos are Australia's largest psittacine species by weight, and they use tools socially. Males perform 'drumming' displays, whereby they bang a fashioned stick against a branch or tree hollow (shown) to produce individualistic drumbeats with rhythm! These remarkable displays aid in territorial defence as well as pair-bonding. (In this image you can see the male holding the stick; the female is below.)

Like other cockatoos, they pair for life and are very long-lived (40–60 years old), but unlike other cockatoos they do not flock.

They mainly occur on Queensland's Cape York Peninsula and in New Guinea, but in both countries their numbers continue to decline. In New Guinea they are hunted unsustainably, and in Cape York they face land-clearing from expanding mining operations, fires that destroy their old (> 250 years) nesting trees, and an extremely low reproductive rate.

Words and photograph: Dr Christina N. Zdenek.

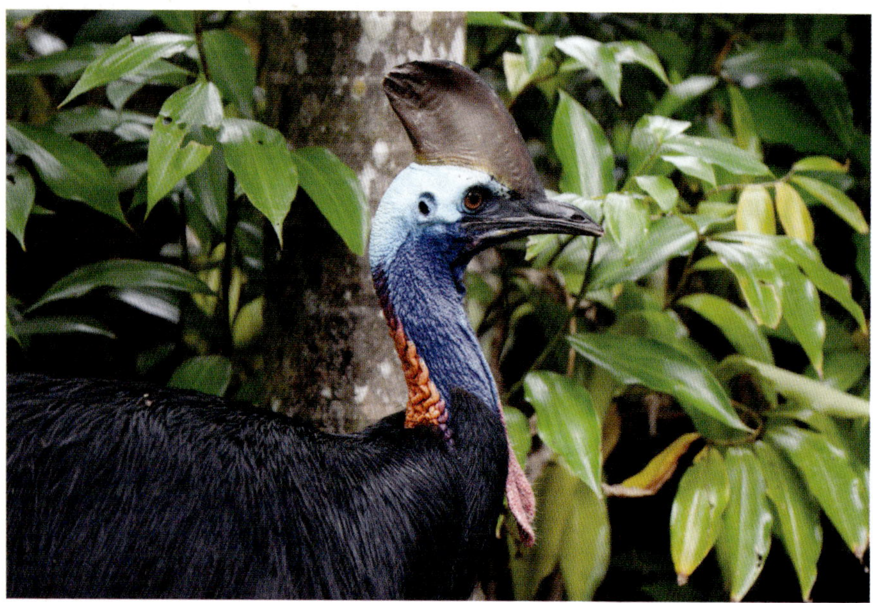

Southern Cassowary

Casuarius casuarius johnsoni

The southern cassowary is the most spectacular of all non-flighted birds, called ratites, with a history of survival that dates back to the age of the dinosaurs. With its substantial casque, or helmet, blue neck and striking red wattles, the cassowary is uniquely colourful in this group of birds. The male takes over all brooding and raising of the young. He not only protects the young, but also ensures they're well fed by dissecting their food into manageable pieces.

This splendid ratite is very important for the survival and diversity of tropical rainforests in northern Queensland and New Guinea. Largely a fruit-eater, it disperses the largest seeds in the forest – something no other animal can do. Indeed, the cassowary distributes over 200 species of seeds in its droppings, often carrying seeds long distances. Some trees can only re-germinate after first passing through the cassowaries' digestive tract. Losing these birds would have dire consequences for the biodiversity of tropical rainforests.

Their habitat is very fragmented, criss-crossed by roads, fences, cars and dogs, but many steps are being taken to help this beautiful bird survive.

Words: Prof. Gisela Kaplan.
Photograph: Prof. Heiko Daniel.

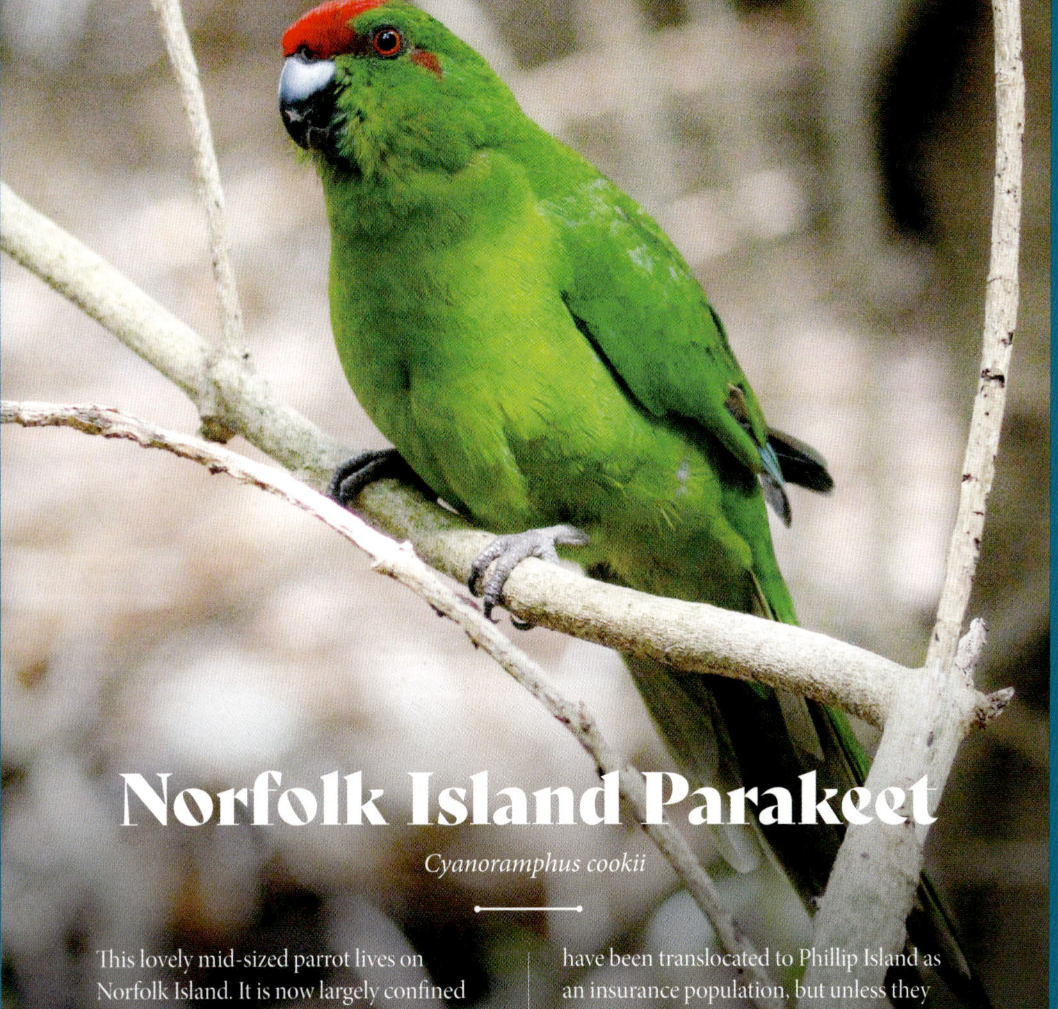

Norfolk Island Parakeet

Cyanoramphus cookii

This lovely mid-sized parrot lives on Norfolk Island. It is now largely confined to the island's national park, where some protection is offered from feral cats and rats, but youngsters that try to leave the park have only a 50/50 chance of survival. Introduced birds such as the crimson rosella, *Platycercus elegans*, also compete for nest hollows.

Once reduced to just 50 pairs, then seeming to recover, its numbers appear to go through cycles of downturns. Some pairs have been translocated to Phillip Island as an insurance population, but unless they are taught to recognise new foods and predators, the new population may fail.

These parakeets have a narrow feeding range, including Norfolk pine, fleshy fruits such as guava and Niau palm, and otherwise seasonally available dry seeds, bark, leaves and flowers.

Words: Prof. Gisela Kaplan.
Photograph: Mick Roderick.

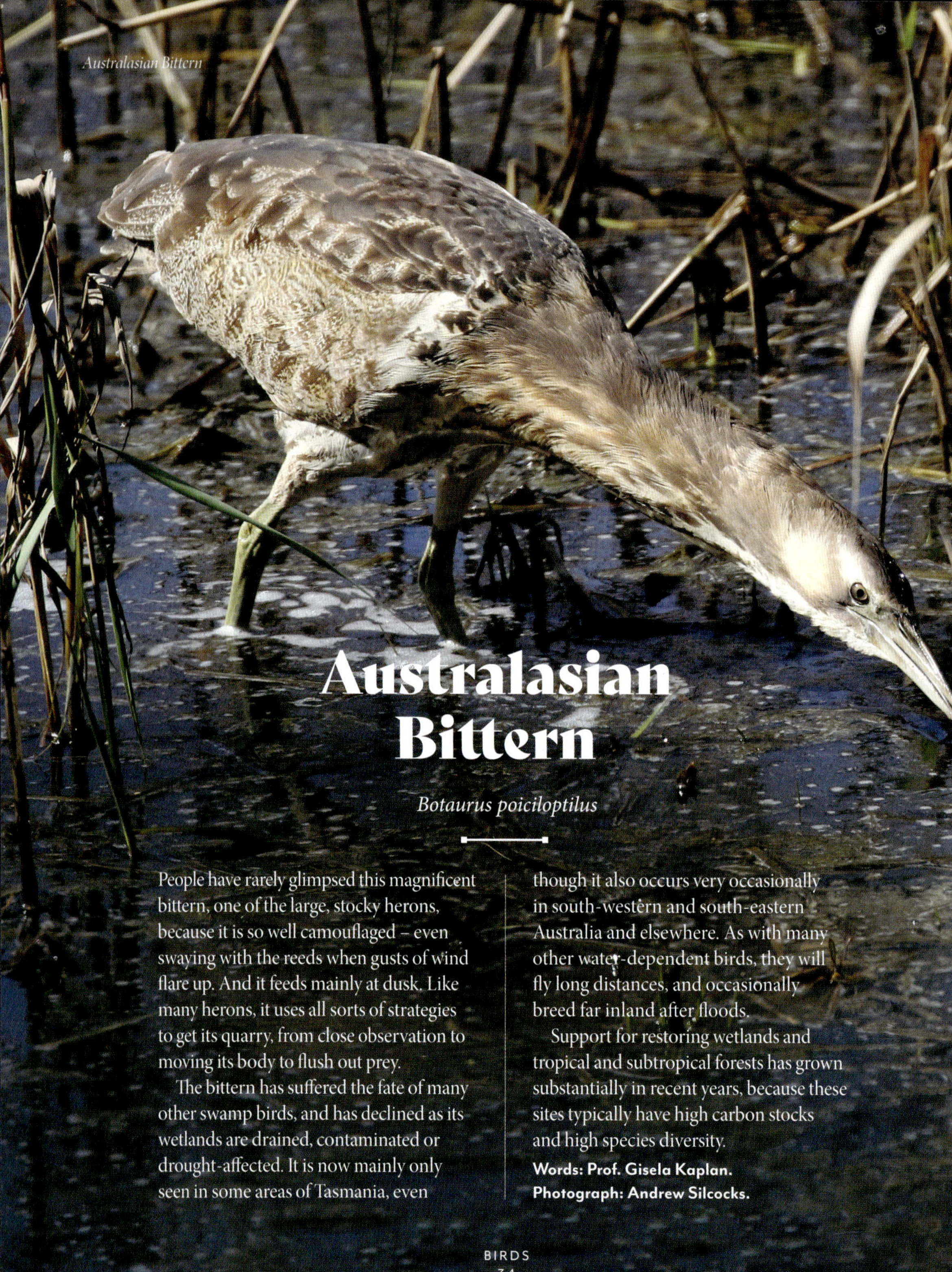

Australasian Bittern

Australasian Bittern

Botaurus poiciloptilus

People have rarely glimpsed this magnificent bittern, one of the large, stocky herons, because it is so well camouflaged – even swaying with the reeds when gusts of wind flare up. And it feeds mainly at dusk. Like many herons, it uses all sorts of strategies to get its quarry, from close observation to moving its body to flush out prey.

The bittern has suffered the fate of many other swamp birds, and has declined as its wetlands are drained, contaminated or drought-affected. It is now mainly only seen in some areas of Tasmania, even though it also occurs very occasionally in south-western and south-eastern Australia and elsewhere. As with many other water-dependent birds, they will fly long distances, and occasionally breed far inland after floods.

Support for restoring wetlands and tropical and subtropical forests has grown substantially in recent years, because these sites typically have high carbon stocks and high species diversity.

Words: Prof. Gisela Kaplan.
Photograph: Andrew Silcocks.

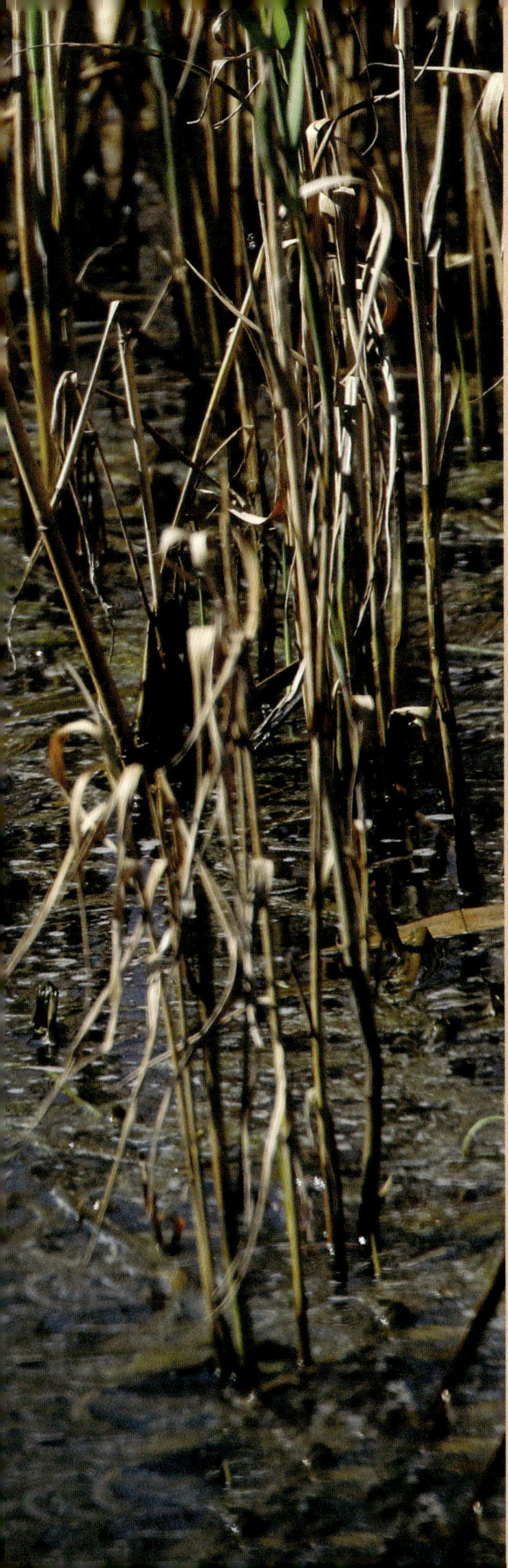

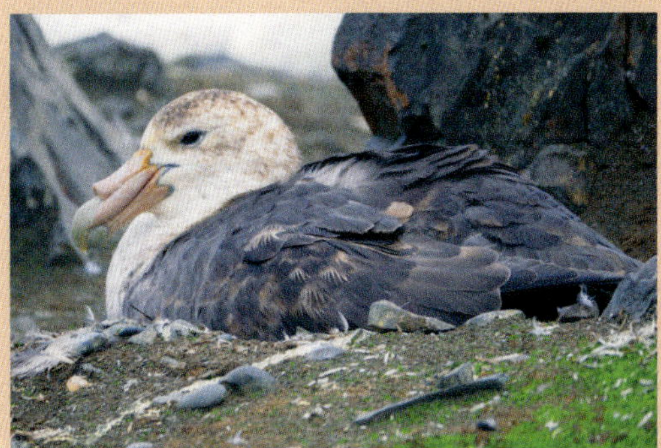

Southern Giant Petrel

Macronectes giganteus

The southern and northern sister species are the largest of the petrels, sometimes also called fulmars – a Norwegian name referring to the foul-smelling substance they expel from their beaks when facing up to a predator. A special adaptation, as in most pelagic birds, is a long nose-tube on top of the bill – it's equipped with a salt gland, and the salt in the solution is expelled via this nose tube.

Southern giant petrels breed in Australian Antarctic territories as well as Macquarie, Heard and McDonald Islands. They occur in two morphs – the one as shown above and an almost-white morph.

They sexually mature at seven years of age, but don't usually breed before the age of 10, which makes their survival difficult. Plus, they lay only one egg. Incubation takes two months, and the youngster is ready to fledge three to four months later. Both parents look after the precious chick.

However, their breeding success depends largely on whether introduced predators, such as rats, are present – rats can kill all the chicks of an entire colony. Other threats include illegal longline fishing, trawling, plastics, and overfishing.

Words and photograph: Prof. Gisela Kaplan.

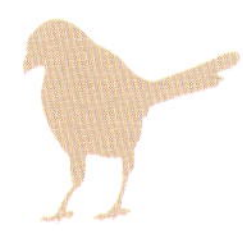

Simon Cherriman

Ornithologist

For over 30 of my 37 years I have had a passionate interest in birds. I enjoyed a cherished childhood that saw me climbing trees, watching birds, and learning first-hand all that I could about these remarkable creatures. I'd keep detailed journals about the nests I found in my backyard and the bush beyond. This led me to pursue a career in science, focusing on ornithology, and later on wildlife photography and film-making which I used to educate and inspire others about the magic of our feathered flying friends.

Birds are well known for their role as bio-indicators, 'canaries in the coalmine' that are living signs of environmental change.

But the more I learned about birds and their biology, the more I learned to read the stories they were telling me. Telling us. About what we were doing to their environment. And unlike most happily-ever-after fairytales, the gossip birds were tweeting about was often dark and bleak.

Birds are well known for their role as bio-indicators, 'canaries in the coalmine' that are living signs of environmental change. The booms in populations of some species, and busts in others, reflect how we've altered ecosystems. Several, like the galah and magpie, are 'ecological winners', having benefited from modified environments more suited to their own needs.

As Australians gradually stripped the native vegetation from this unique landscape, replacing old-growth trees with farmland, and expanding urban areas into forests, hills and heathland, many birds began to suffer. Their lost habitat meant fewer places to nest and forage, and introduced predators had increasingly easy access to feathered foods. The application of a European mindset to a country managed for tens of millennia by Aboriginal People saw nine species go

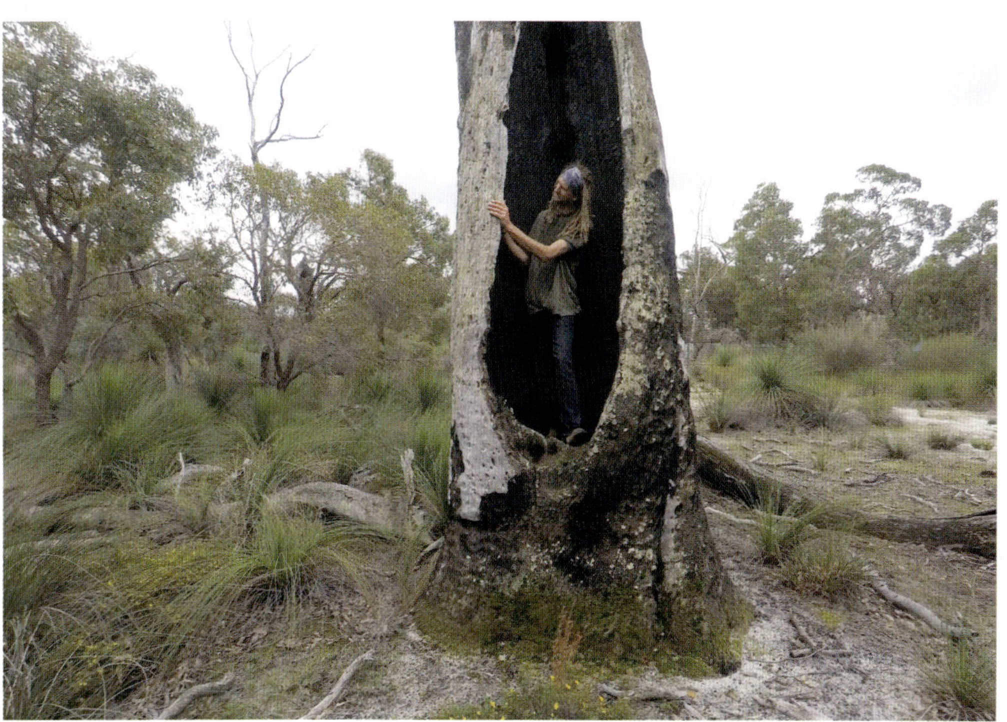

extinct, with an increasing number added to the 200-plus Threatened taxa.

Nature is made up of many different parts, with each working together to make the whole thing healthy. And like your body, when some of those parts are lost – or become extinct – the whole thing loses health and can't function normally. Birds play critical roles in keeping our environment – and therefore, us – alive.

What can we do? When we humans get sick, we seek advice from a doctor. So, when the land is sick, we need to consult the 'doctors' of our environment – ecologists and environmental scientists. These people tell us that the best treatment for our land and birdlife is to restore lost habitats and encourage biodiversity back.

How? Firstly, we can support the multitude of existing organisations that are already set up to help save populations of Threatened species. Then, we can become better custodians of the spaces in which we live – our backyards and bush reserves – to preserve and/or plant local native plants, control weeds, and strive to keep them pest (and pesticide) free.

As birdlife returns and ecosystems recover, we will be rewarded for such healthy work with increasingly assorted, celebratory songs. Nature's music soothes even the most savage of beasts.

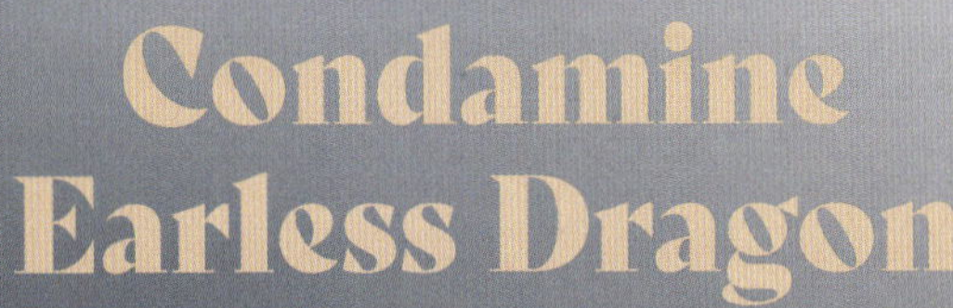

Condamine Earless Dragon

Tympanocryptis condaminensis

Croplands stretch to the horizon on the fertile plains of Queensland's Darling Downs. This is part of the nation's food bowl. It is also the only habitat left for the dumpy little Condamine earless dragon, with its striped pattern and prickly skin. Narrow grassy verges are all that remain of the grasslands it used to occupy. Native grasses have been replaced by maize, sorghum and cotton. Fortunately, the local farmers use a practice of 'minimum till', where the soils are not deeply ploughed, and this seems to favour the little dragons, which are clinging on – but only just – in the modified environment.

Words and photograph: Steve Wilson.

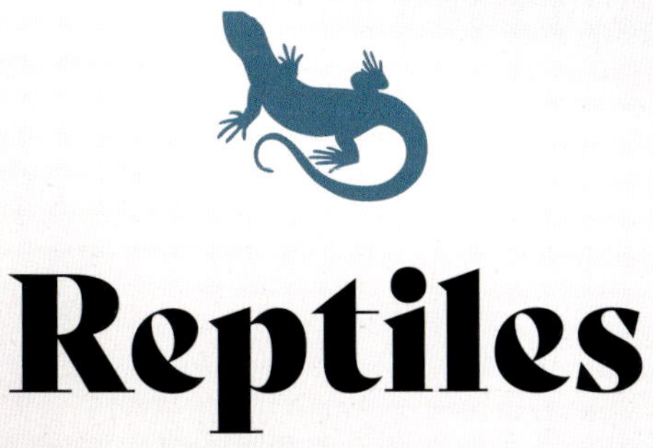

Reptiles

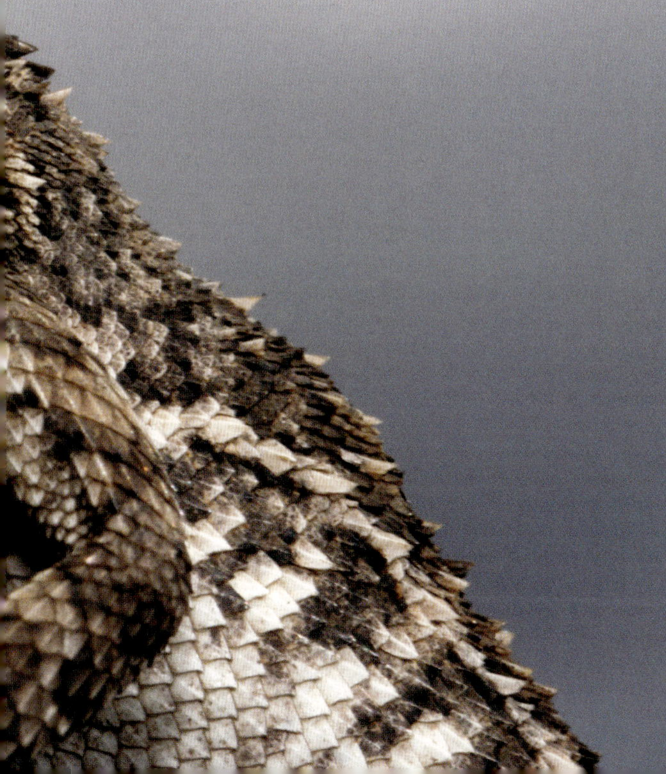

Broad-Headed Snake

Hoplocephalus bungaroides

Broad-headed snakes are victims of their own unique character and beauty. For decades they have been prized by reptile collectors as terrarium exhibits, causing severe declines in some populations. They are most vulnerable to collectors during winter and spring, when they shelter under flat sandstone slabs on rock pavements atop cliffs and escarpments in the Sydney area.

Slabs have been broken, or turned and not replaced by over- zealous snake hunters. Bush rock has also been removed for garden decorations. Artificial rocks moulded from cement have been placed at some sites to recreate that critical shelter. Fortunately for the snakes, however, parts of their habitat include inaccessible ledges on cliff faces.

Words and photograph: Steve Wilson.

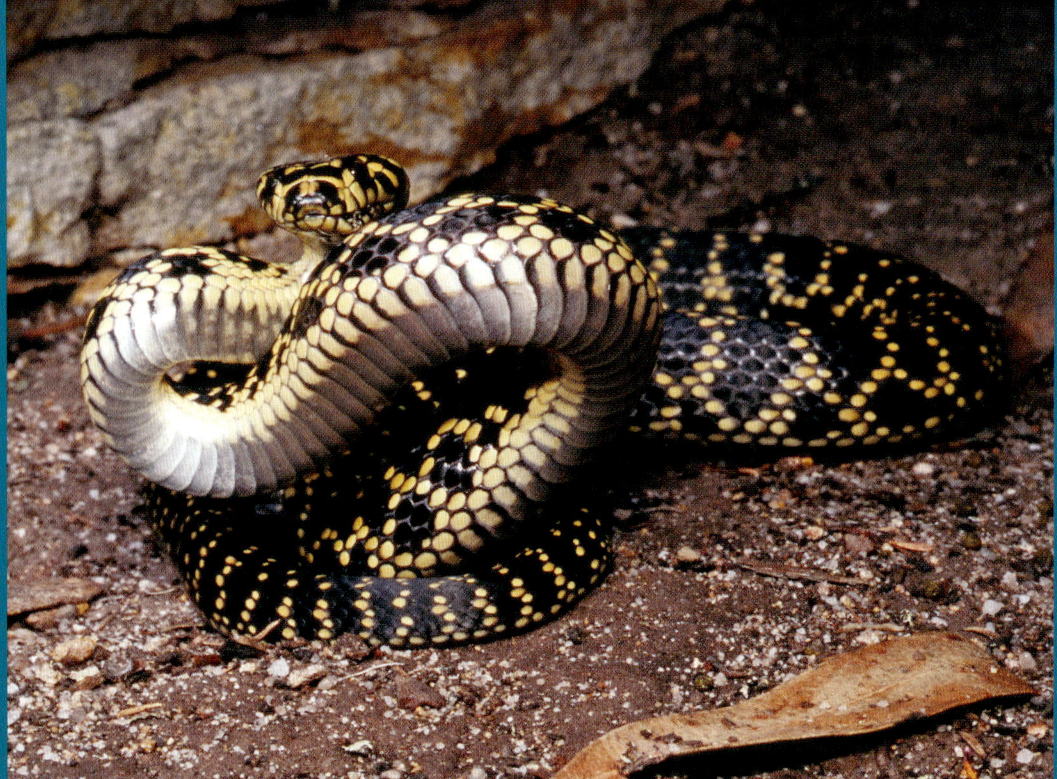

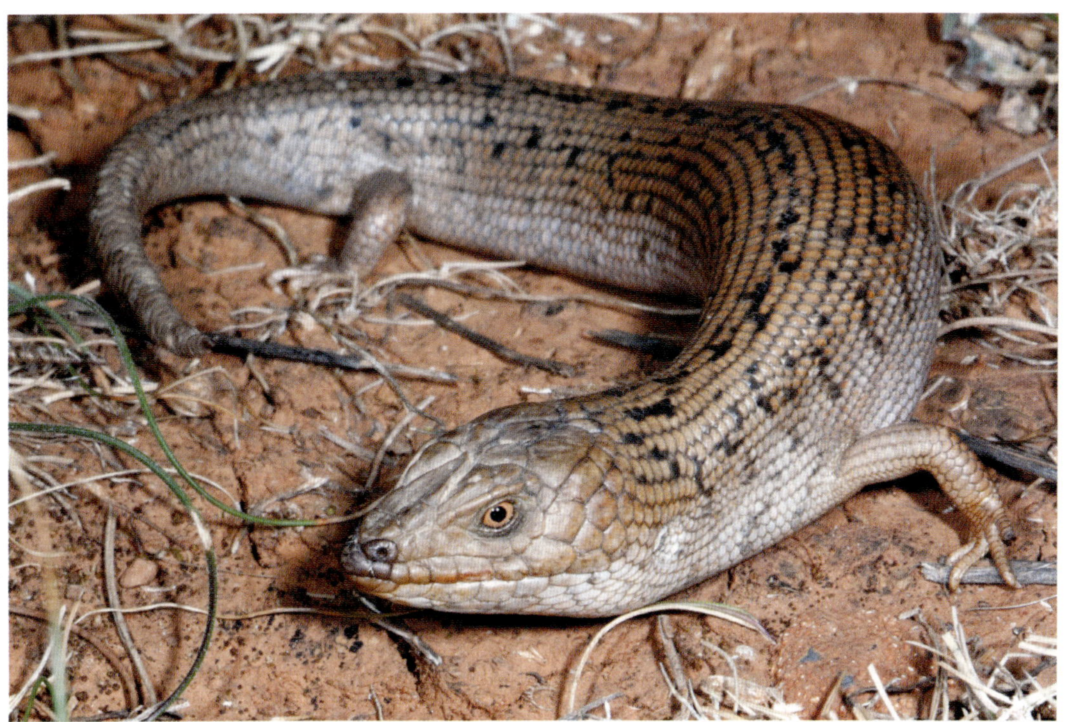

Pygmy Blue-Tongue

Tiliqua adelaidensis

We thought we had lost the pygmy blue-tongue. Not seen for decades. Extinct. That was until the 1990s, when some curious naturalists investigated the lump in a road-killed brown snake, and were astonished to discover what it had eaten! The search was on for a live one in treeless grasslands near Burra, South Australia. It turns out these secretive lizards were hiding under our noses, living in vertical trapdoor spider holes. Their big sturdy heads can block the burrow shaft, yet their slender, flexible bodies can turn around in the confined space. They seldom stray far, ambushing invertebrate prey from the burrow entrance. **Words and photograph: Steve Wilson.**

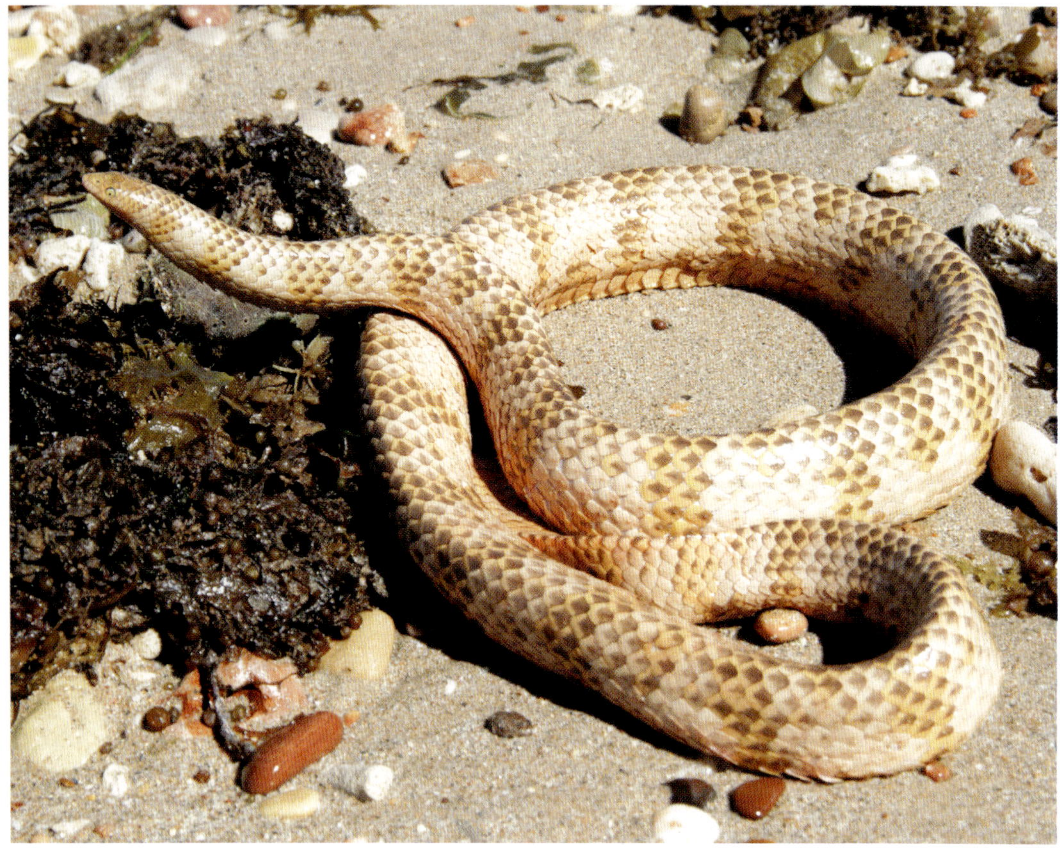

Short-Nosed Sea Snake

Aipysurus apraefrontalis

Although it was feared extinct by 1998, this species was rediscovered in 2015, and is now known to have two distinct populations: an oceanic, seemingly deeper water population at Ashmore and other reefs in the Timor Sea, and a coastal population from Western Australia, between Exmouth and Broome. Based on differences in genetics, morphology and ecological parameters, these two populations could potentially be distinct species from one another. In some parts of their coastal range, short-nosed sea snakes are often caught as bycatch in the prawn trawler industry, which is most likely the major threat to this species.

Words and photograph: Dr Ruchira Somaweera.

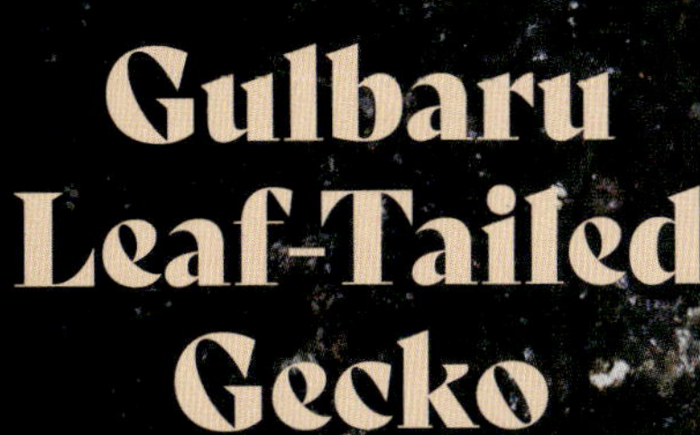

Gulbaru Leaf-Tailed Gecko

Phyllurus gulbaru

In the vine thickets of the Hervey Range near Townsville in northern Queensland, the granite boulders are flecked and dotted with minerals. These boulders are home to Gulbaru leaf-tailed geckos. Their backs and limbs are marked exactly like the background and their skin is adorned with prickly scales, so the lizards are virtually invisible against the rocks. By day they hide in crevices and at night they forage for insects over the exposed surfaces.

But the geckos have a problem. Their distribution is confined to a tiny area, and their habitat has been fragmented by clearing and threatened by encroaching fires and advancing weeds.

Words and photograph: Steve Wilson.

Blue-Tailed Skink

Cryptoblepharus egeriae

Endemic to Christmas Island, blue-tailed skinks were found all over the isle until the 1990s, when introduced predators including the wolf snake and the giant centipede ravaged the population.

Recognising a dramatic decline in the species, Christmas Island National Park staff captured 66 blue-tailed skinks before initiating a captive breeding program in 2010, which has been hugely successful in boosting their numbers and has brought them back from the brink of extinction.

In 2019, 300 blue-tailed skinks were translocated to the predator-free island of Pulu Blan, in the Cocos (Keeling) Islands group, which has allowed the species to return to the wild after having been in captivity for a decade. At this stage a return to the wild on Christmas Island is still not possible, due to the presence of introduced predators.

Words and photograph: Wondrous World Images.

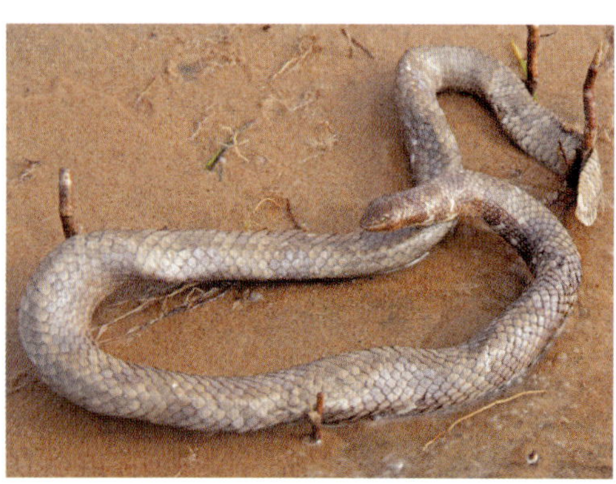

Leaf-Scaled Sea Snake

Aipysurus foliosquama

Sadly, this is an image of a dead leaf-scaled sea snake from a research survey. This species is similar to the short-nosed sea snake, and was also considered extinct from its only known range in the Timor Sea. But recent studies have confirmed breeding populations at Shark Bay in Western Australia, with additional records from Barrow Island and other places along the Pilbara coast. At Shark Bay, it is common in the bycatch of the prawn trawler industry, and is Critically Endangered.

Words and photograph: Dr Ruchira Somaweera.

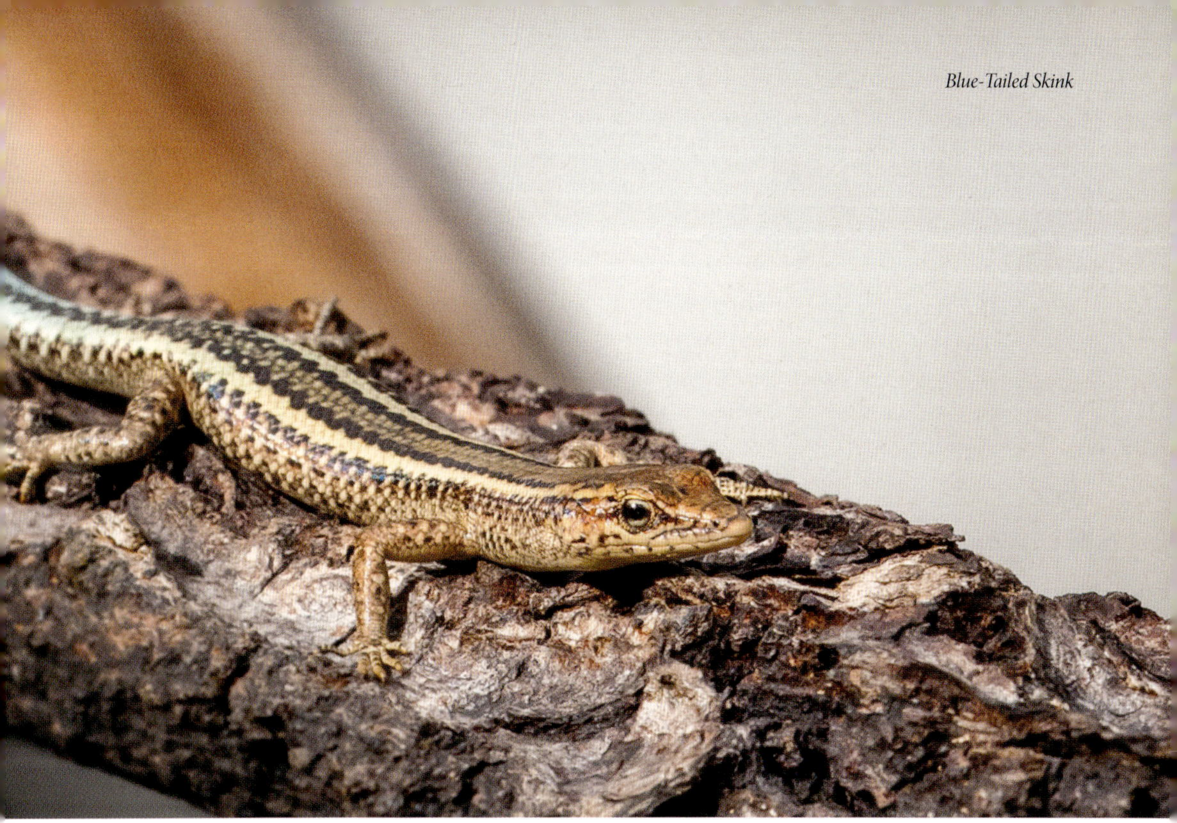

Blue-Tailed Skink

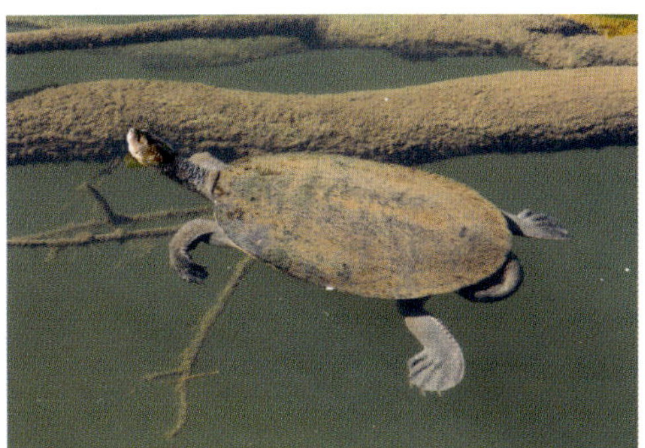

Mary River Turtle

Elusor macrurus

This turtle was known as the pet shop turtle, long before anything was learned of its ecology. It was only named in 1994, yet it's our largest freshwater turtle! We now know it is restricted to the Mary River system north of Brisbane. Males have large fleshy tails, more than half the length of the shell. And this is one of the 'bum-breathing' turtles, able to supplement oxygen intake by drawing water into its cloaca. Adults are long-lived and persist in the wild, but juvenile recruitment is falling due to predators. Community groups are now protecting nests and incubating eggs to rear and release young. **Words and photograph: Steve Wilson.**

The Bellinger River Turtle

Myuchelys georgesi

In 2015, the Bellinger River turtle was pushed to the brink of extinction by a novel virus, which killed almost all the adult turtles in the river. Occurring only within the Bellinger River drainage – a restricted range on the North Coast of NSW – the species was formerly locally abundant. Today as few as 150 Bellinger River turtles remain however, making them one of the world's 25 rarest turtle or tortoise species.

Their ability to recover hinges on the success of captive breeding programs at several zoos, but threats such as predation by foxes and hybridisation with other species of turtle in the river remain. This 45-million-year-old turtle needs your help. Citizen scientists in the area can record any turtle sightings using the TurtleSAT app.

Words: Ricky Spencer.
Photograph: Aussie Ark.

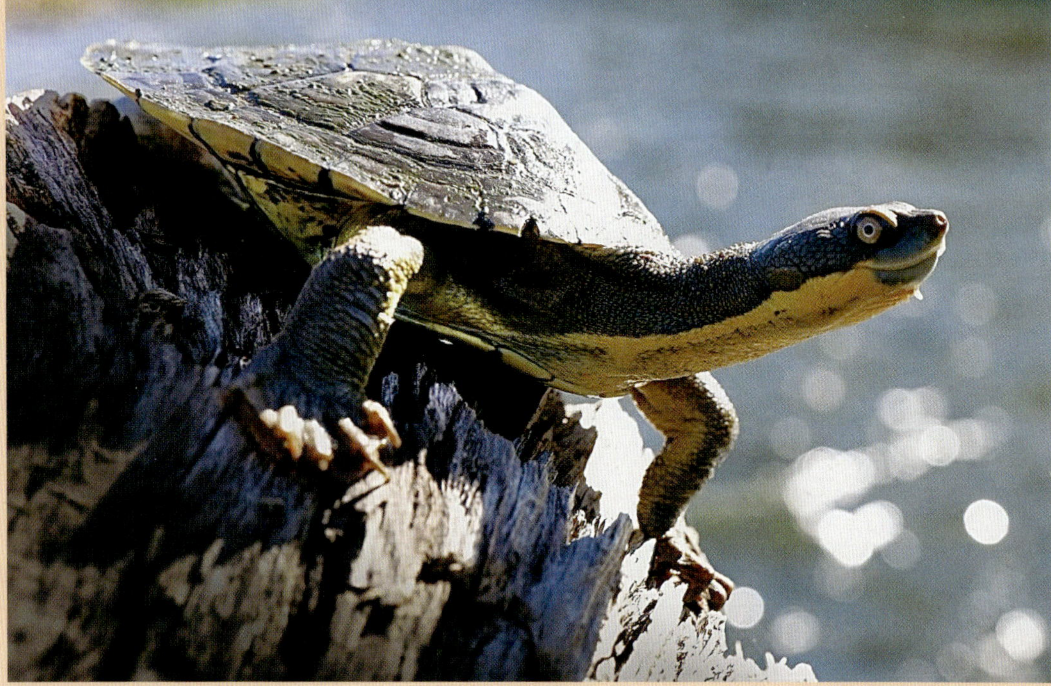

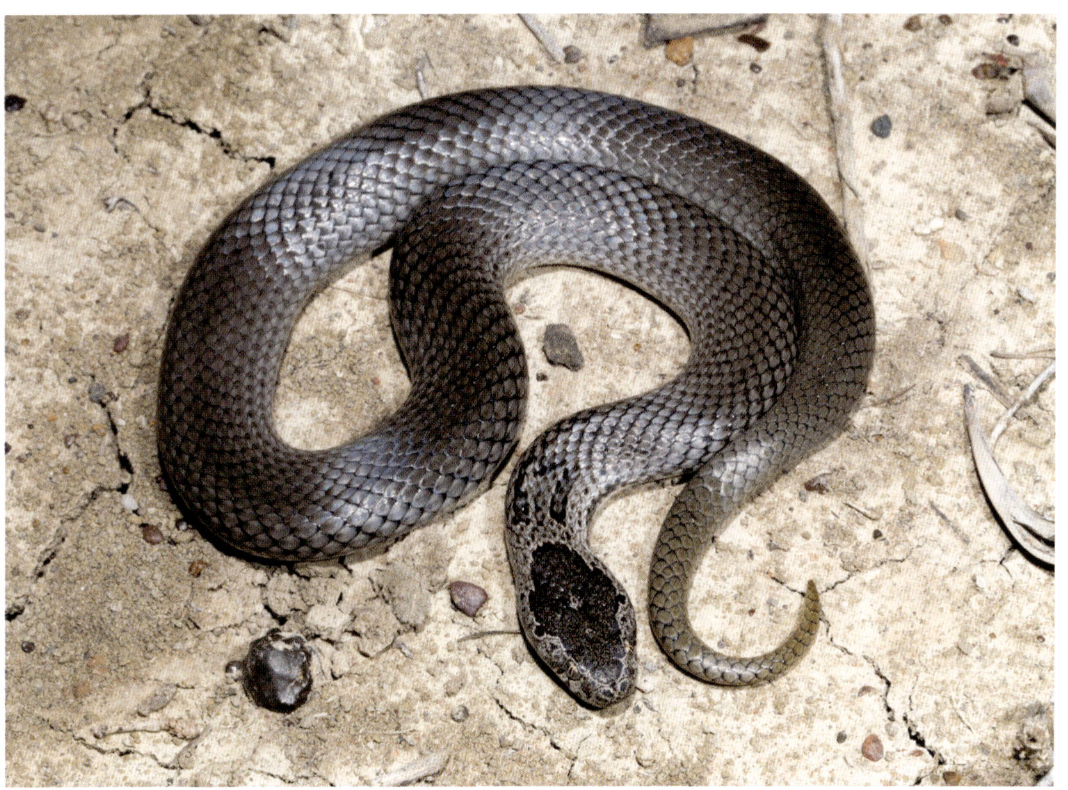

Ornamental Snake

Denisonia maculata

Deep in the cracking clay soils in Queensland's northern Brigalow Belt, frogs are tucked away during the long, hot dry period, waiting for torrential rain. When it falls, it fills depressions called gilgais or 'melon-holes', triggering thousands of frogs to emerge. Up come the ornamental snakes too.

These venomous snakes specialise in eating frogs. They occur in fragmented pockets of high density, where clay soils are seasonally flooded. Where the soils change and the landscape rises, their numbers drop off sharply.

Their habitat is also prime pastoral land, extensively cleared, compacted and pock-marked with deep hoof prints. Coal and gas are increasingly playing a role in land use here, with open cut mines and a spaghetti of buried pipelines. Small wonder ornamental snakes are regarded as Vulnerable.

Words and photograph: Steve Wilson.

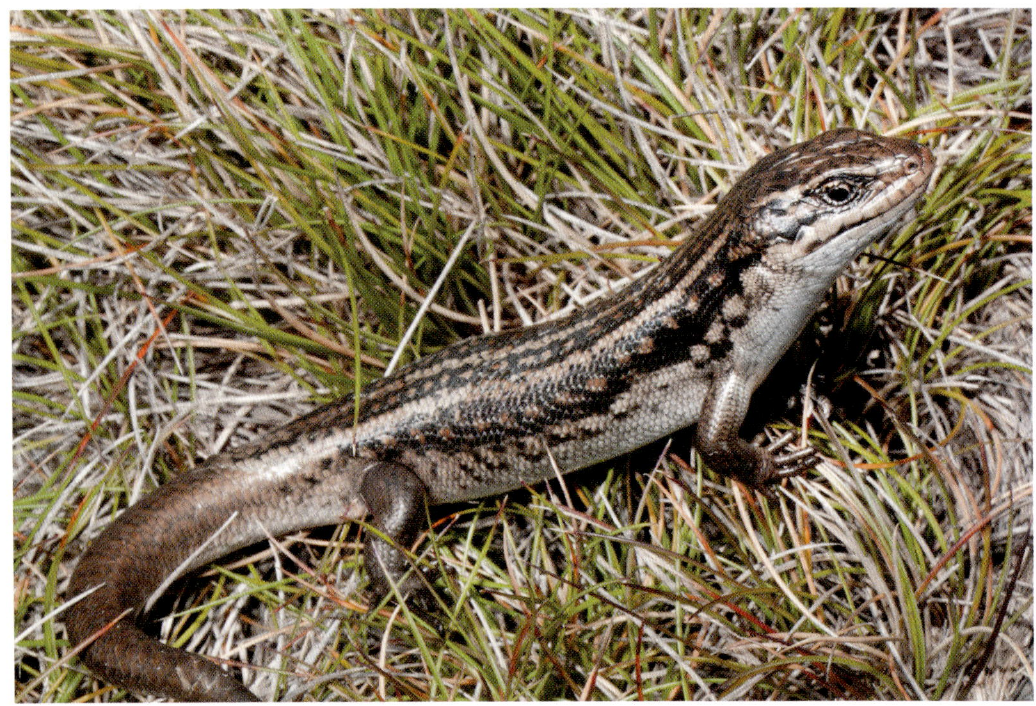

Guthega Skink

Liopholis guthega

Guthega skinks live in small colonies, excavating shallow burrows under rocks, logs and shrubs in alpine and subalpine zones. During winter inactivity, soil and snow cover act as important buffers against extreme cold. They are believed to have small home ranges, remaining close to familiar burrows and basking sites.

High altitude living has consequences though, with much of their habitat fragmented and populations separated by distances greater than their dispersal ability. Cleared and modified terrain on ski slopes and alpine resorts, feral animals such as horses, the spread of weeds, increased fires and higher temperatures, all combine to threaten Guthega skinks.

Words and picture: Steve Wilson.

Loggerhead Turtle

Caretta caretta

Australia is just part of the wide distribution of Loggerhead Turtles, but it does harbour extremely significant breeding sites. On select beaches such as Mon Repos in Queensland, generations of female turtles have hauled their great bulk up the sand, dug deep burrows for their precious eggs, and carefully covered them over before returning to the sea.

Today's generations face a raft of new threats, including discarded nets, chemical and plastic pollution, and overfishing. On land, their eggs and their young fall prey to pigs and foxes. And hotter sand, warmed by climate change, affects the gender balance of offspring, creating a bias to males.

Words and photograph: Steve Wilson.

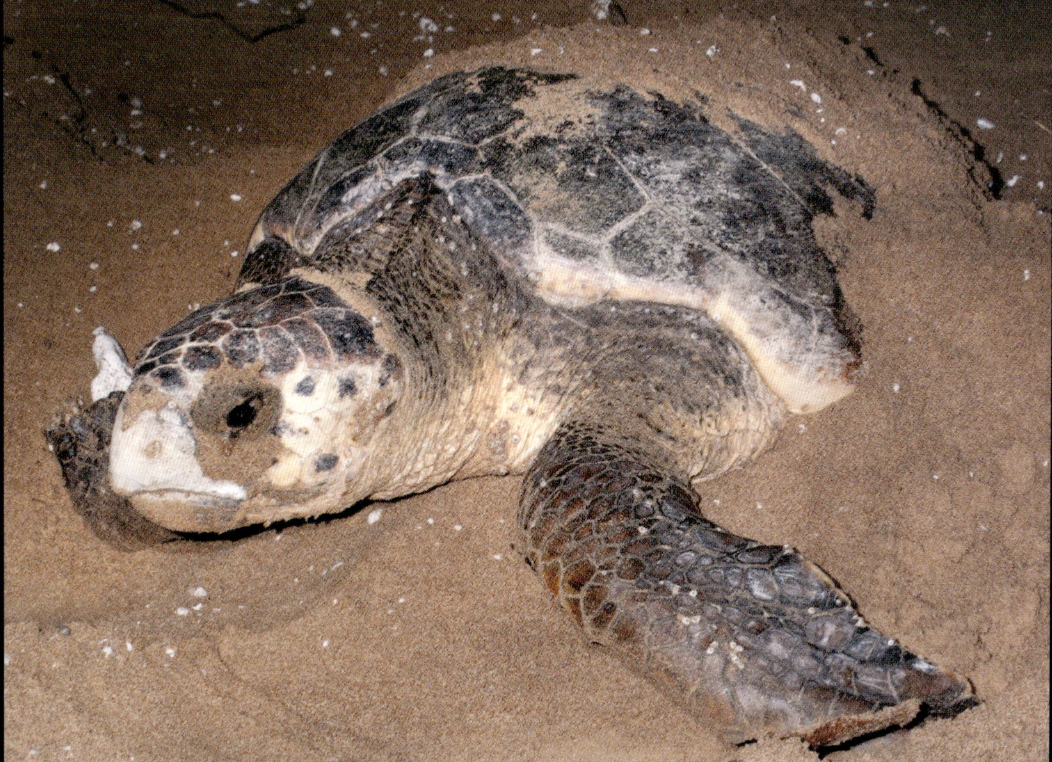

Western Swamp Turtle

Pseudemydura umbrina

In 1953, a Western Australian schoolboy took a turtle to a pet show. It turned out to be a long-lost species, named in 1901 but overlooked and forgotten. This curious little turtle is confined to tiny isolated seasonal swamps, baked dry in summer and fed by winter rains, on the plains north of Perth.

Numbers of western swamp turtles in the wild dropped from hundreds in the 1970s to about five in the late 1980s. Foxes, rats and summer fires are the likely culprits. They are Critically Endangered, but captive breeding has been successful, along with predator-proof fencing. Turtles have now been reintroduced to old sites, and new populations have been established where the habitat looks suitable and secure.

Hard work and research are holding extinction at bay. Just!

Words and photograph: Steve Wilson

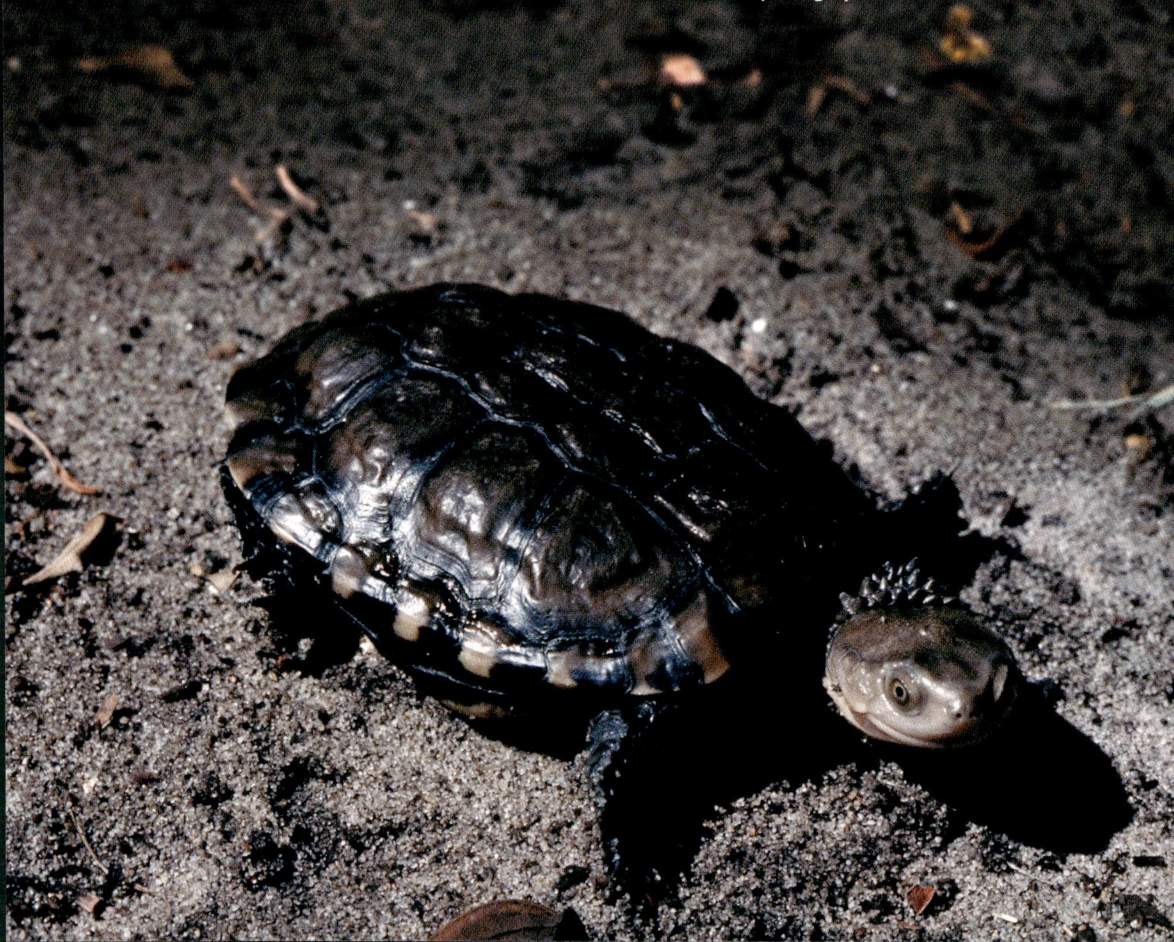

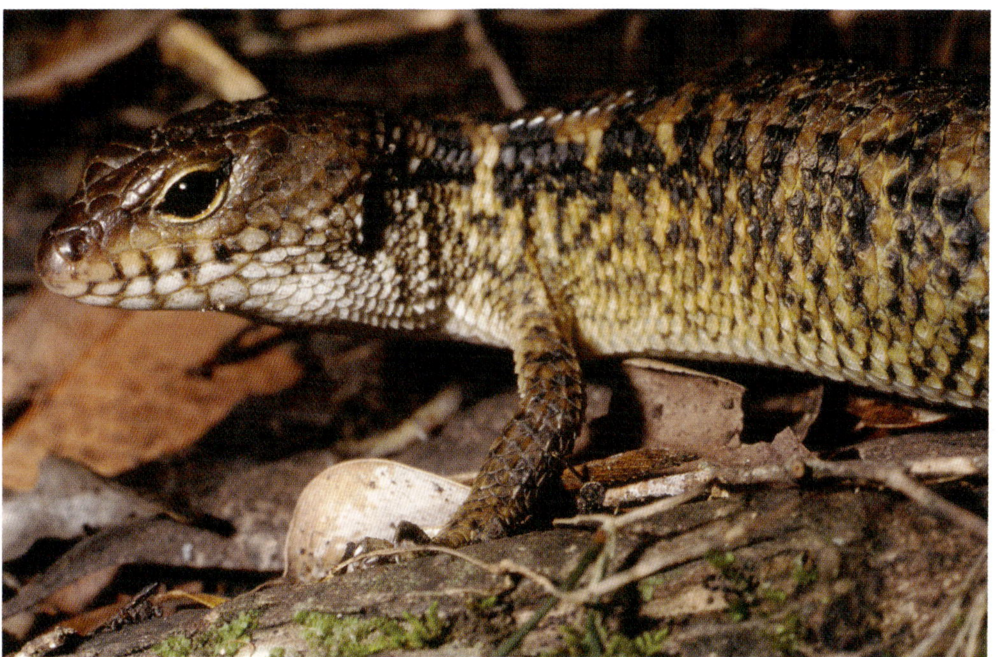

Nangur Skink

Nangura spinosa

Nangur skinks live in permanent burrows excavated in the heavy soil at the base of trees, vines and rocks in dense vine scrub. They seldom leave these burrows, preferring to rest partly exposed on a flat earth platform at the burrow entrance. It's not really an action-packed regime, but it works well to ambush passing invertebrates!

Just two populations exist, about 60km apart, in south-eastern Queensland. Once threatened by logging, they are now living in protected areas, but there is a real risk of weeds like lantana and cat's claw smothering the burrow entrances and interfering with their basking activities.

Words and photograph: Steve Wilson.

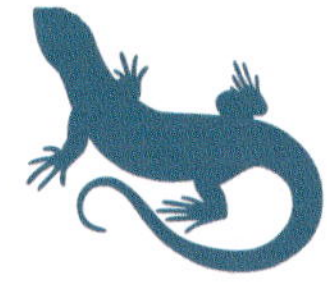

Steve Wilson

Herpetologist, naturalist, photographer and author

I've been passionate about reptiles since I could walk. With a lifetime of observing, photographing and documenting reptiles comes a stockpile of rich memories of the snakes, lizards and turtles that have crossed my path. Those early excursions after school to hunt skinks at the local creek in suburban Melbourne are still as clear as a bell. So too are recollections of my parents indulging my interest with outings to my choice of reptile-rich destinations.

A relentless passion can be a double-edged sword, but it has taken me over most of Australia and to some spectacular centres for biodiversity around the world. It has been a privilege to pursue my interests, and I feel endowed with a great wealth, measured in treasured experiences.

Yet something of those memories now preys on my mind. Looking back over the years I recall a strong element of abundance. The constant rustling in the leaf litter as skinks made noisy dashes for cover. The sleek glossy texture of a red-bellied black snake as it moved gracefully over the coiled bodies of those basking beside it. Counting the bearded dragons perched on fence posts from the car window. The splashing 'plop... plop... plop' noise made by turtles dropping from their perches as I walked along the river bank.

The animals I accepted as common and reliable, even including the skinks in my own backyard, are getting thinner on the ground.

I don't see much of that abundance these days, and I wonder about myself. Is that really the way it was, or am I looking back with rose-coloured glasses? Or am I losing my edge? Is a dulling of my sharp ears and keen eye-sight causing me to overlook the animals I would have seen when I was younger?

I don't think so. Surveys in Queensland's Brigalow Belt are confirming what I have been suspecting for some time. Intensive searches with teams of ecologists in outwardly intact bushland with few

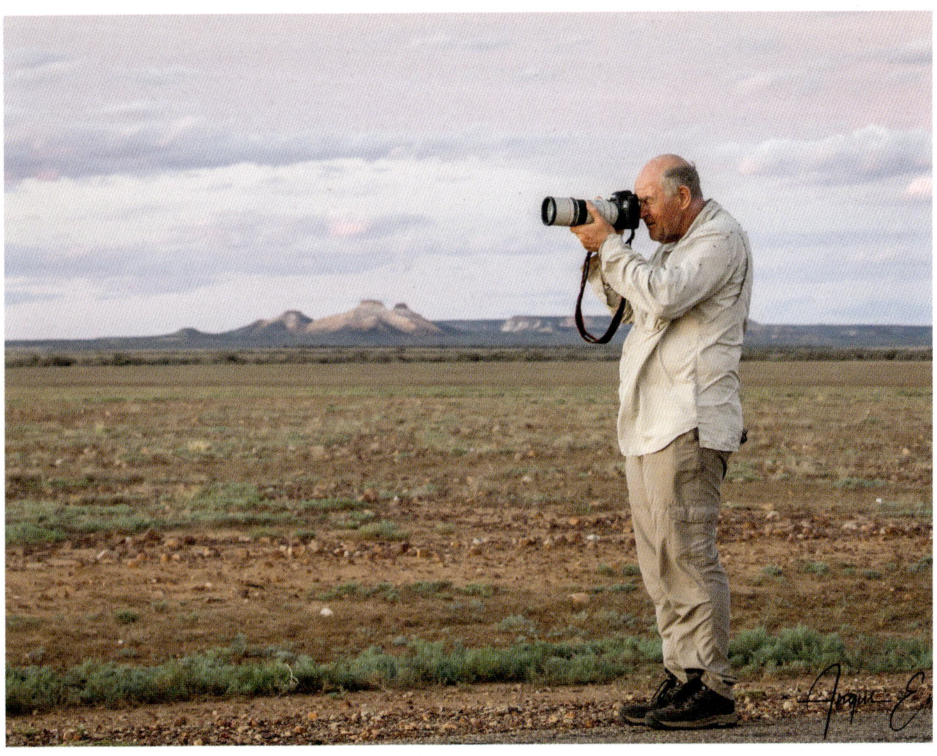

invasive species and no recent burns during great weather is revealing very little. The leaf litter has been largely silent. Then I remember the droughts and the heatwaves of just a couple of years ago, when there were months without rain and temperatures in the 40s. And there were the ones in preceding years. I'm starting to think those extreme weather events have sucked the life out of these places. They may look green now, but abundance has become scarcity.

I now believe this has been going on for some time. The animals I accepted as common and reliable, even including the skinks in my own backyard, are getting thinner on the ground. If lots of skinks were rustling in that leaf litter, I would have heard them! I think we are experiencing the first negative impacts of a changing climate on Australian biodiversity. I know there are still areas where reptiles of all kinds remain common, but if those parts of Queensland I have been studying intensively for the past several years are symptomatic of a bigger picture, then this is something we need to deal with as a matter of urgency! Of course, the first step is acceptance that research-based science trumps social media as our most reliable information sources.

Photograph: Angus Emmott.

Leafy Sea Dragon

Phycodurus eques
Weedy Sea Dragon:
Phyllopteryx taeniolatus

The leafy and weedy sea dragons are related to the seahorse, and are endemic to Australia's temperate waters. Male sea dragons carry the eggs fixed to the underside of their tail, unlike seahorses, that have a pouch for rearing young.

The leafy sea dragon is listed as Near Threatened on the IUCN Red List of Threatened Species. The weedy sea dragon is protected by state legislation in NSW and Tasmanian waters, and listed as Data Deficient.

Sea dragons have been recognised as a species most threatened by over-collecting through the aquarium trade. Australian sea dragons are not currently used in traditional ethnic medicine, although dried and powdered sea dragon has been found for sale.

Other major threats to sea dragons include pollution and excessive fertiliser run-off, as well as the loss of their coastal habitats, including seagrass and seaweed.

Words and photograph: Justin Gilligan.

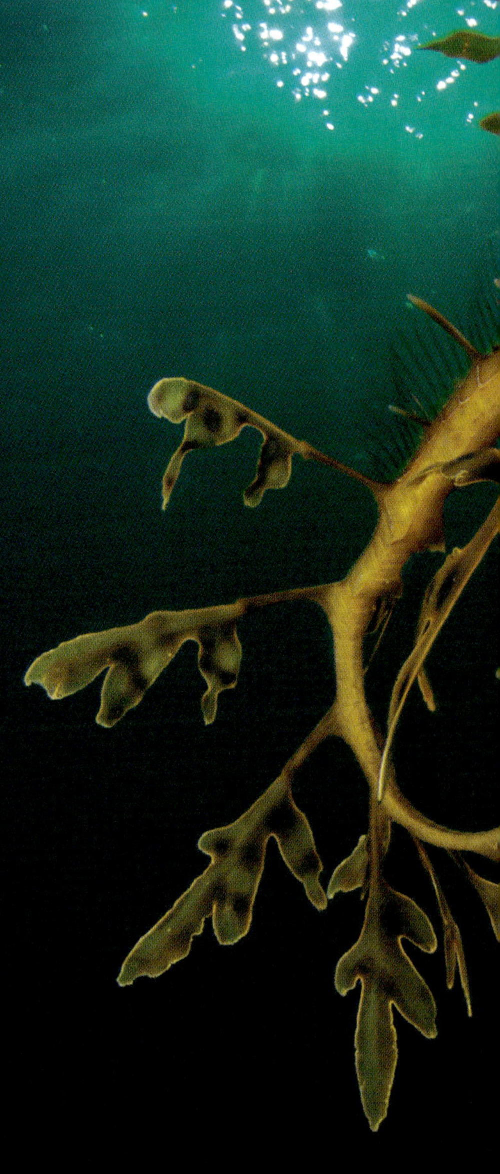

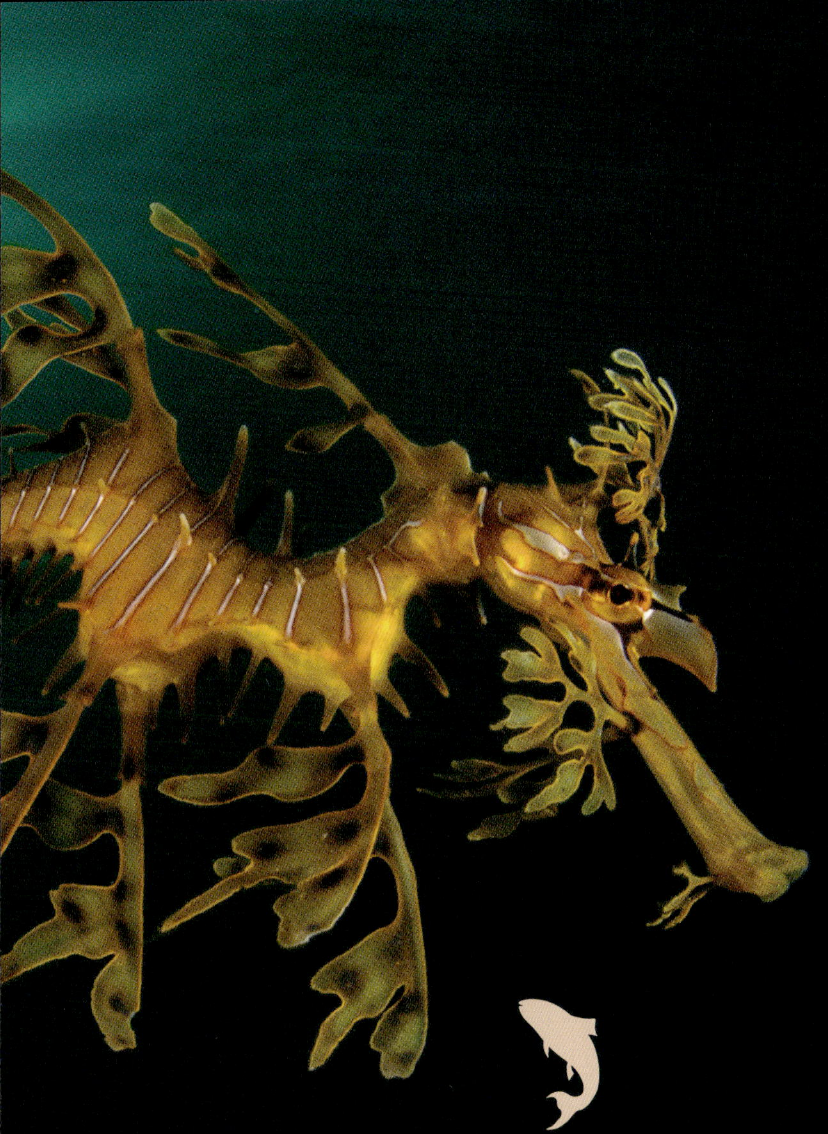

Fish, Crustaceans & Echinoderms

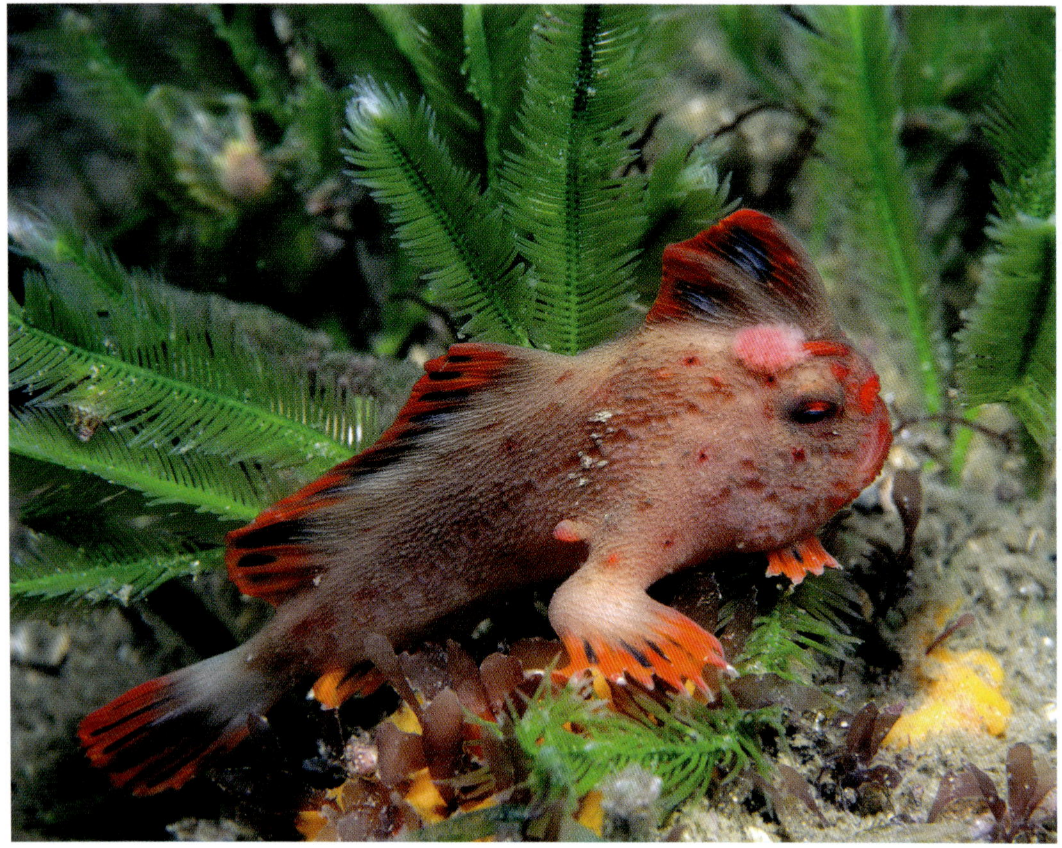

Red Handfish

Thymichthys politus

The red handfish is one of the rarest marine fishes in the world – there are likely only around 100 individuals left.

Instead of swimming, this fascinating fish walks on its fins over the sea floor. This is a joy for anyone to see – especially as the fins look like human hands. It is found in only two small 50m-long patches of reef in south-eastern Tasmania.

The Handfish Conservation Project has been established in an effort to protect the red handfish from extinction in the wild.

Words: Dr Kerstin Bilgmann.
Photograph: Gary Bell/oceanwideimages.com.

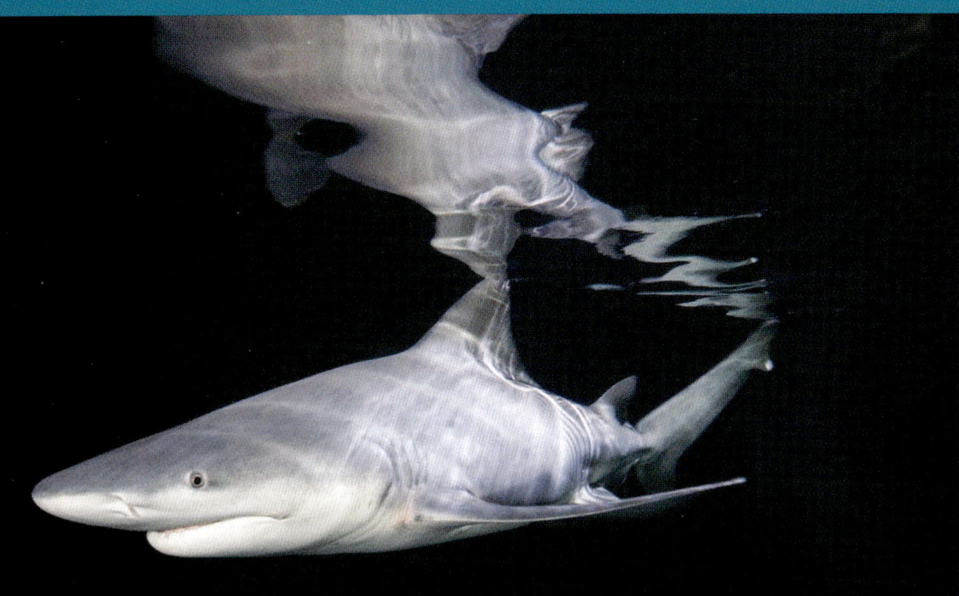

Speartooth Shark

Glyphis glyphis

The speartooth shark lives in tidal rivers and estuaries of the Northern Territory and Queensland. It has recently been discovered to also occur in the Kimberley region of Western Australia. Juveniles and sub-adults live in murky rivers, while adults move to coastal marine waters. Their teeth in the upper and lower jaw are of different shape, and some of their bottom teeth are spear-shaped, which is how they got their name.

Although they look scary, they don't pose a risk to humans – but humans pose a risk to them. In fact, their biggest threats are human activities, particularly fishing and habitat modification. They were thought to be naturally rare, so it is exciting that more of them have recently been discovered – but they are still a threatened species.

Words: Dr Kerstin Bilgmann.
Photograph: SEA LIFE Melbourne.

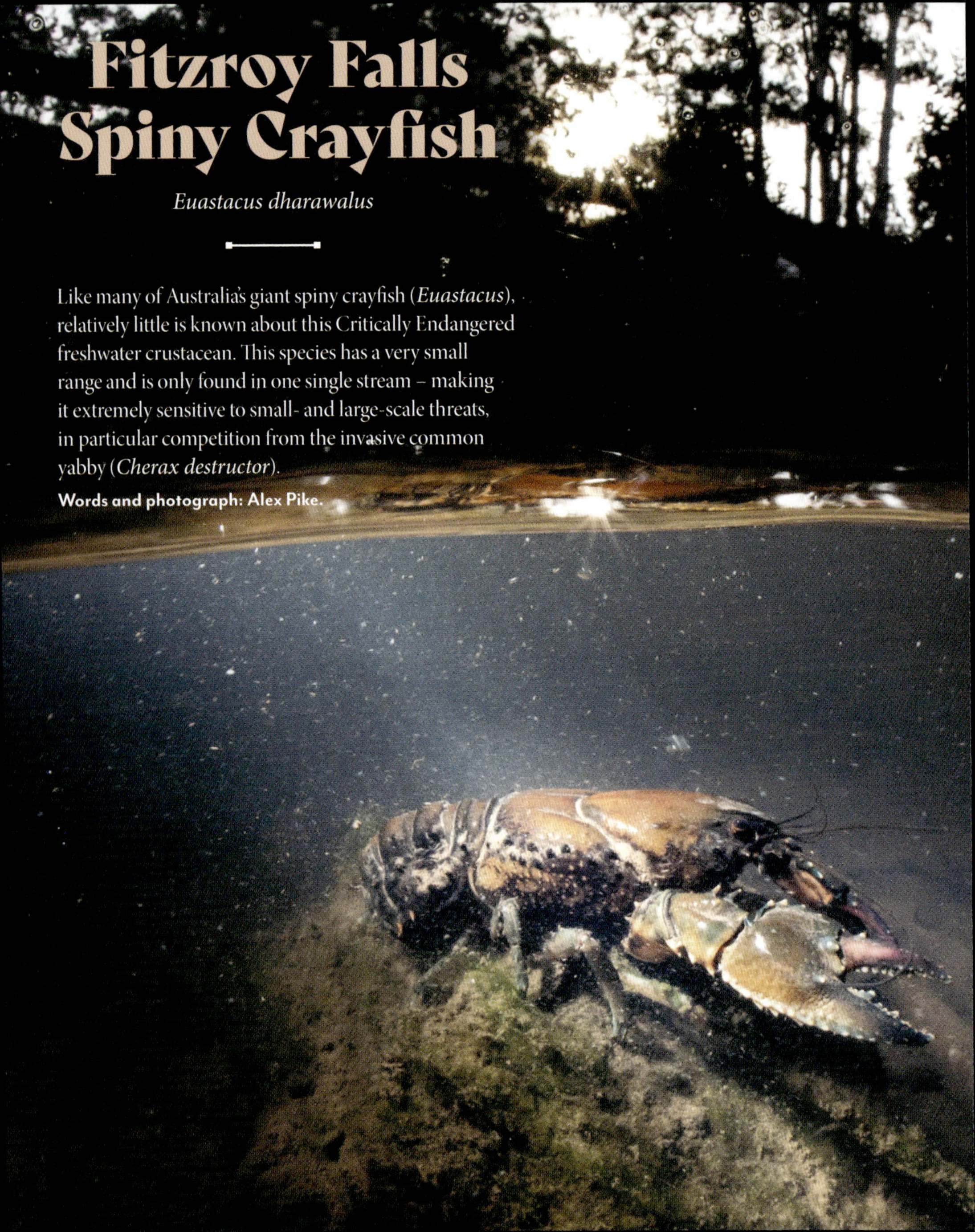

Fitzroy Falls Spiny Crayfish

Euastacus dharawalus

Like many of Australia's giant spiny crayfish (*Euastacus*), relatively little is known about this Critically Endangered freshwater crustacean. This species has a very small range and is only found in one single stream – making it extremely sensitive to small- and large-scale threats, in particular competition from the invasive common yabby (*Cherax destructor*).

Words and photograph: Alex Pike.

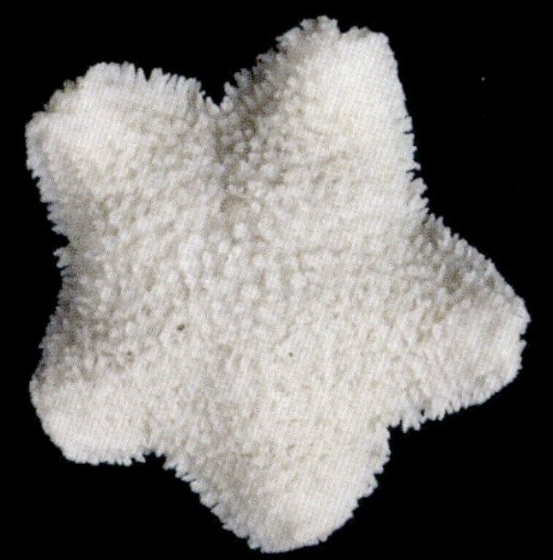

Derwent River Seastar

Marginaster littoralis

This small seastar is a mystery. It has not been seen for years, and it is highly likely that we've lost this species entirely and it has become extinct. But no one knows for sure. The Derwent River seastar is known from only five locations in the Derwent River near Hobart, Tasmania. The Tasmanian Museum and Art Gallery holds a few preserved specimens, collected between 1969 and 1991.

What may have caused its disappearance? It is thought that the invasive New Zealand seastar caused it, by either taking over the habitat or genetically swamping the Derwent River seastar by hybridising with it. The New Zealand seastar was accidentally introduced to Tasmania in the early twentieth century.

Words: Dr Kerstin Bilgmann.
Photograph: Blair Patulo/Museum Victoria.

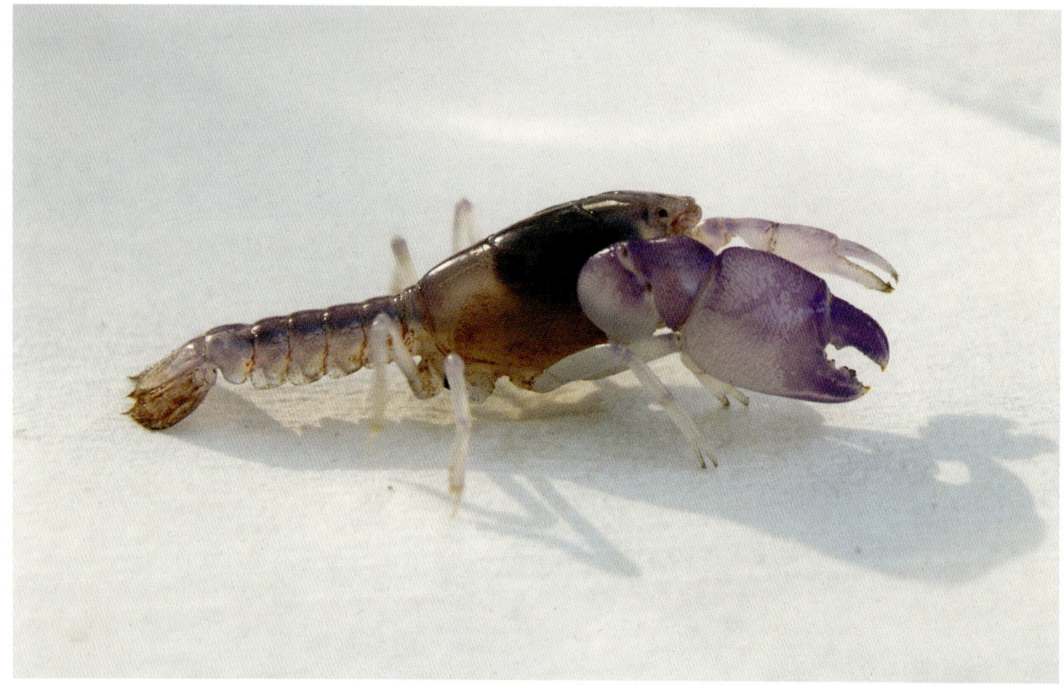

Dunsborough Burrowing Crayfish

Engaewa reducta

The Dunsborough burrowing crayfish is only known from two regions in Western Australia – near Dunsborough and Margaret River. It digs expansive burrow systems in swamps and near creek lines. The burrows can be several metres deep.

This freshwater crayfish hardly ever surfaces, and is only seen when conditions are very wet. If you find a sandy chimney in the swamp you might be on its track, but after some rainfall these may just look like unrecognisable piles of sand. Because this species looks almost identical to two other burrowing species – the Margaret River and the Walpole burrowing crayfishes – it can easily be confused with them. Disappearing swamp habitat poses the biggest risk to the survival of this species.

Words: Dr Kerstin Bilgmann.
Photograph: Dr Quinton Burnham.

Silver Perch

Bidyanus bidyanus

The silver perch is found in lakes, rivers and reservoirs in south-eastern and eastern Australia. Females lay up to 500,000 eggs each year. It was once one of the most widespread fish in the rivers of the Murray–Darling Basin, but underwent an extreme decline due to overfishing and habitat modification. It's now only sparsely distributed across its range, and is extinct in the Australian Capital Territory. Thankfully, a variety of conservation measures have facilitated the perch's survival, but the species is highly reliant on these endeavours and is still Critically Endangered.

Words: Dr Kerstin Bilgmann.
Photograph: Gunter Schmida/Museum Victoria.

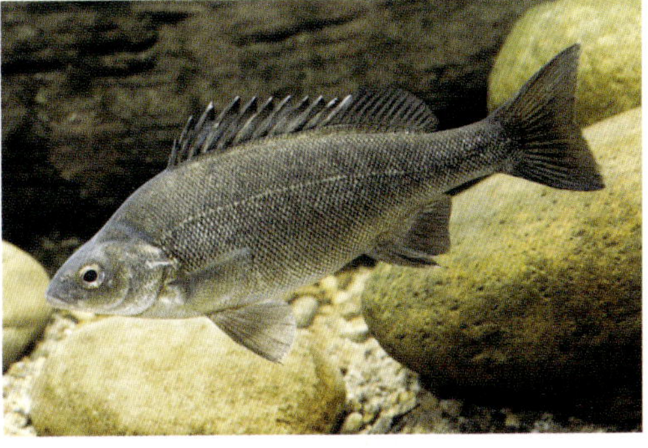

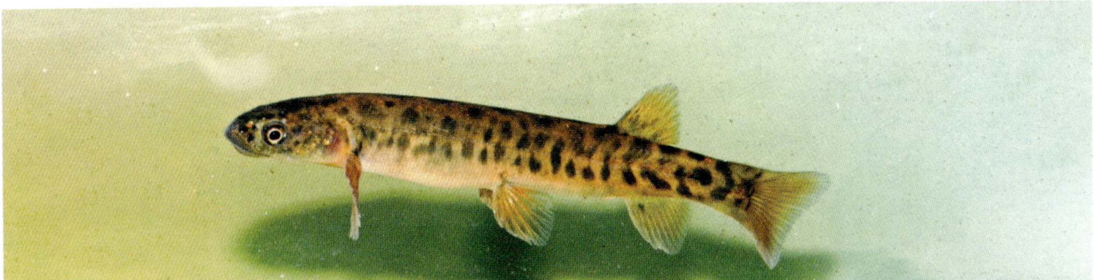

Pedder Galaxias

Galaxias pedderensis

The Pedder galaxias is a small freshwater fish from south-western Tasmania. It was originally only found in Lake Pedder and Lake Maria, but is now extinct in the wild.

When humans flooded Lake Pedder in 1972 to harness energy, the species started to decline rapidly. To save it, some individuals were translocated, and their future survival depends on keeping these new waters free from introduced fish species. Lake Pedder no longer has suitable habitat for the Pedder galaxias, because the flooding introduced predatory brown trout and climbing galaxias, which have taken over.

Words: Dr Kerstin Bilgmann. Photograph: Rudie H. Kuiter/Museum Victoria.

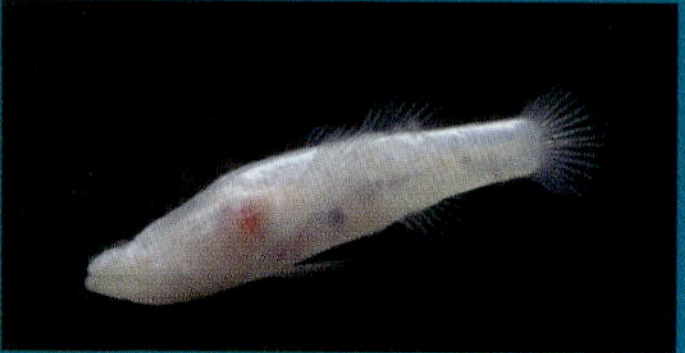

Blind Cave Gudgeon

Milyeringa veritas

Three species of Australian fish have adapted to live in underground aquifers and cave systems, often 30m deep underground. Because they live in the dark, they have no eyes, so rely on sensory papillae on the body to move around and locate food. One of them, the blind cave gudgeon, is found in underground waters beneath the Cape Range Peninsula in Western Australia. This species is listed as Vulnerable, and is likely under threat due to the habitat changes caused by lowering the water table, mining and construction, and pollutants.

Words and photograph: Dr Ruchira Somaweera.

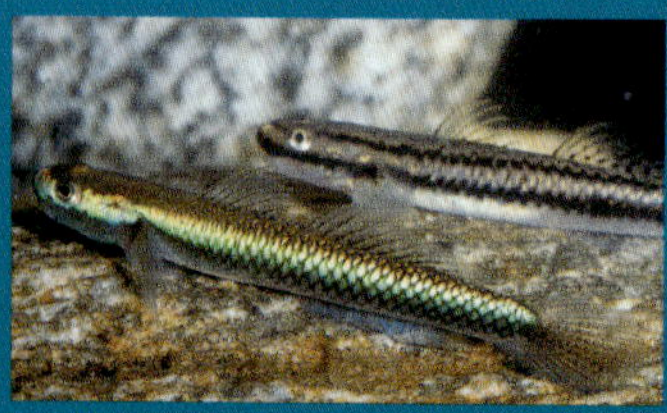

Opal Cling Goby

Stiphodon semoni

This freshwater goby is very rare in Australia. Males have a blue, green or pink shiny colour that changes in the light, while females are whitish and have two black bands. The opal cling goby is found in rainforest streams in far north-eastern Queensland, but there are likely only a few individuals left. Because of its beautiful appearance, it's at risk of being collected illegally.

Words: Dr Kerstin Bilgmann.
Photograph: Dr Gerald R. Allen/Museum Victoria.

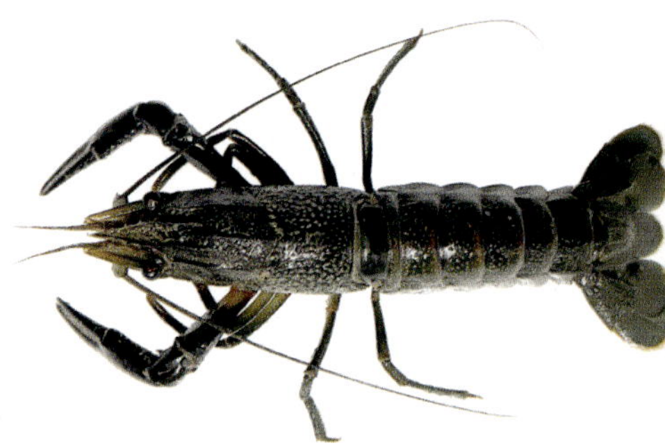

Hairy Marron

Cherax tenuimanus

The hairy marron is a freshwater crayfish that can grow up to 40cm in length. It likes deep river waters and, unlike other freshwater crayfish, does not burrow tunnels in the clay. The hairlike structures on its body led to its name.

The hairy marron has undergone a steep population decline. It is found only in a few locations of the Margaret River in south-western Western Australia. Direct competition and hybridisation with the introduced and more abundant smooth marron make it difficult for it to survive. Illegal fishing also poses a real risk.

Conservation efforts to save the hairy marron include captive breeding and the removal of the smooth marron from key habitat.

Words: Dr Kerstin Bilgmann.
Photograph: Andrew Beer.

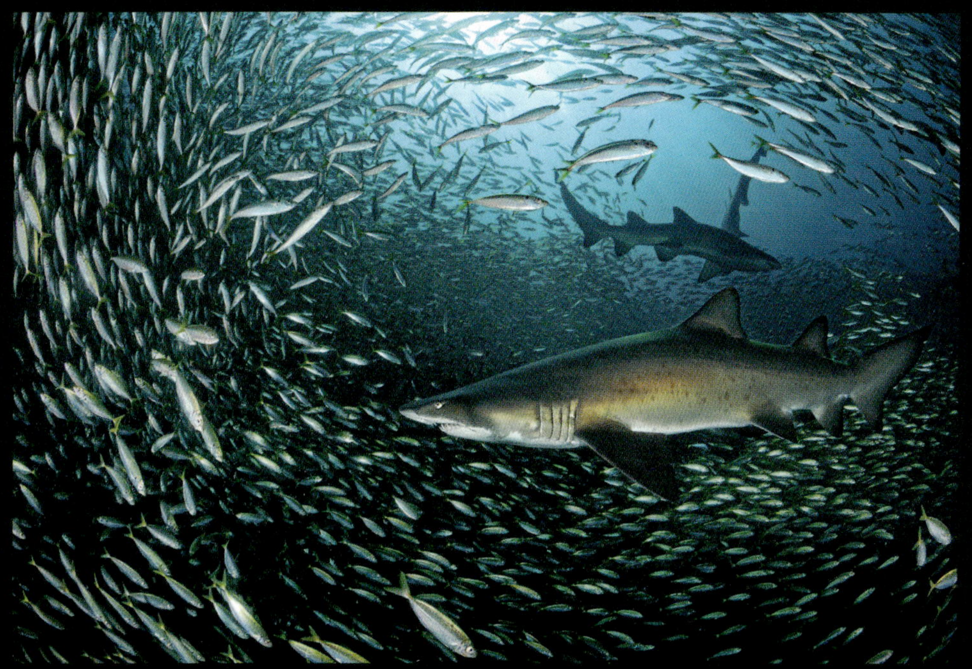

Grey Nurse Shark

Carcharias taurus

Globally, the grey nurse shark is listed as Critically Endangered. Two populations exist in Australia – an east coast population and a west coast population. Their liver oil was used to fuel the lamps that illuminated Sydney streets during the early 1900s, and during the 1960s and '70s divers wielding spears with exploding tips hunted these sharks for sport. Their aggregating behaviour made them easy targets.

Concern about the conservation status of grey nurse sharks was raised in the 1980s, resulting in the species becoming protected in NSW in 1984. Despite this status, grey nurse sharks are now listed as a Critically Endangered species in NSW, and Critically Endangered by the Commonwealth's Environment Protection and Biodiversity Conservation Act 1999. Although positive steps towards their conservation have been achieved, they continue to be caught as fisheries bycatch, and in swimmer shark nets as they seasonally migrate.

Words and photograph: Justin Gilligan.

Spotted Handfish

(Brachionichthys hirsutus)

The spotted handfish is a rare and unusual fish endemic to Australian waters. It has highly adapted pectoral fins, which appear to be like hands and allow it to walk on the sea floor. It was the first marine fish to be listed as Critically Endangered by the IUCN Red List in 1996, and has since maintained that status. Its distribution is restricted to an area around the Derwent River in Tasmania. An introduced species called the Northern Pacific seastar (*Asterias amurensis*) poses the greatest threat to this species, preying on its eggs and also on the sea squirts or ascidians that form the substrate for the eggs.

Since the seastar, native to Japanese waters, was established in the Derwent River and estuary in the 1980s, efforts have been made to control its spread.

Words and photograph: Justin Gilligan.

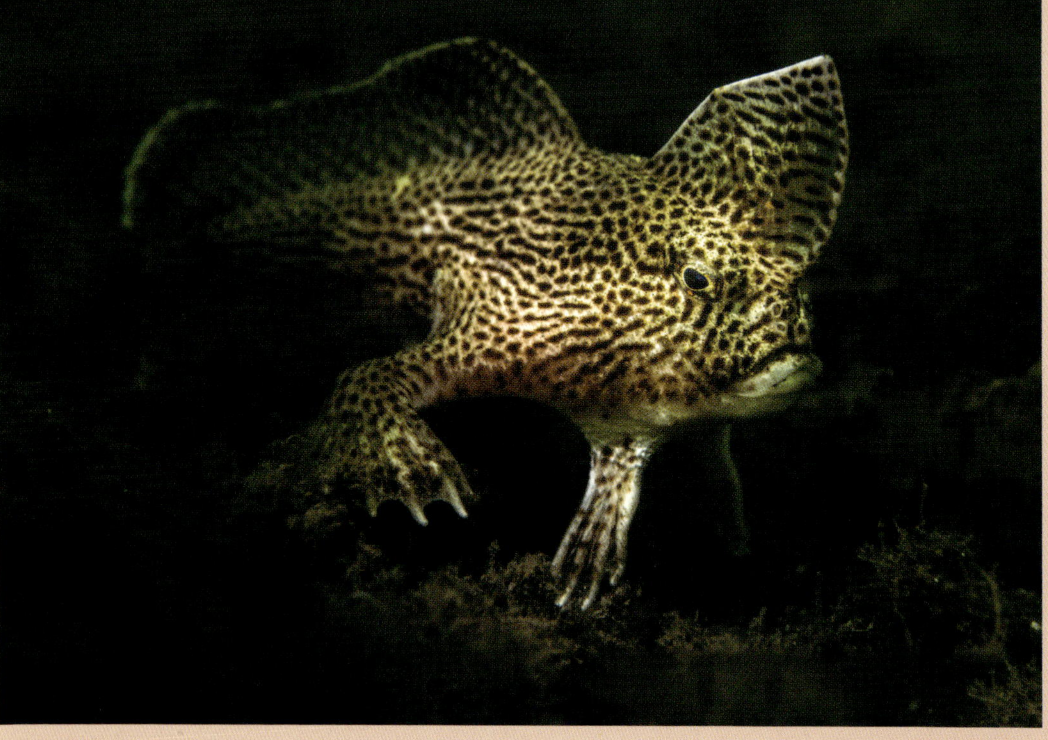

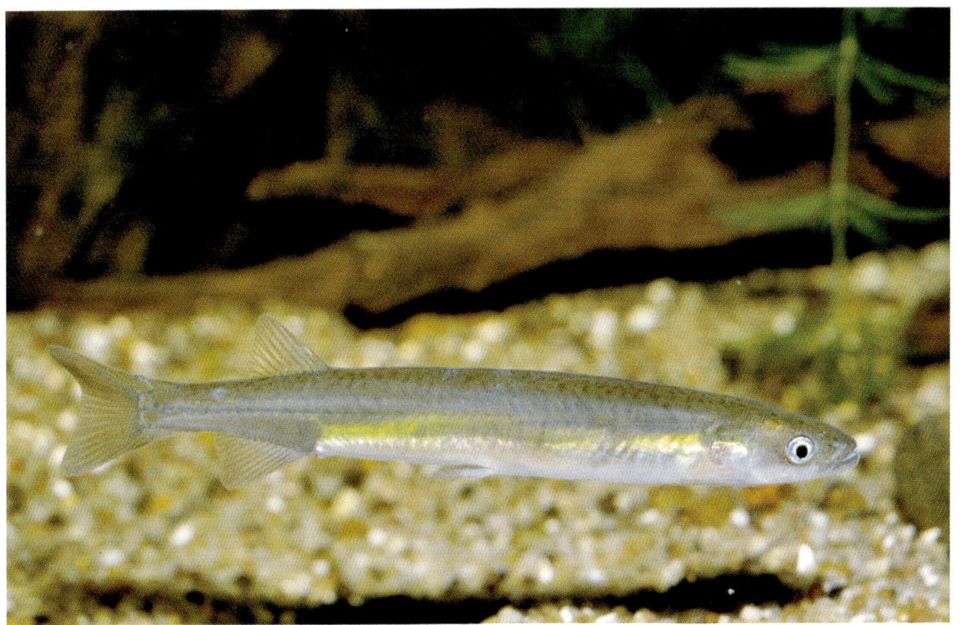

Flathead Galaxias

Galaxias rostratus

With its olive green body, flat head and large mouth, this fish it perfectly adapted to still and slow-moving freshwater bodies. It blends in well with rocky, sandy and aquatic vegetation bottoms. The loss of aquatic plants like ribbon weed is likely a main contributor to its dramatic decline, but human-caused water modifications and introduced species that compete with or predate on this fish also put their survival at risk. The species is now extremely rare, and has recently only been found in two billabong and lagoon areas in the Murray–Darling river system.

Words: Dr Kerstin Bilgmann. Photograph: Neil Armstrong/Museum Victoria.

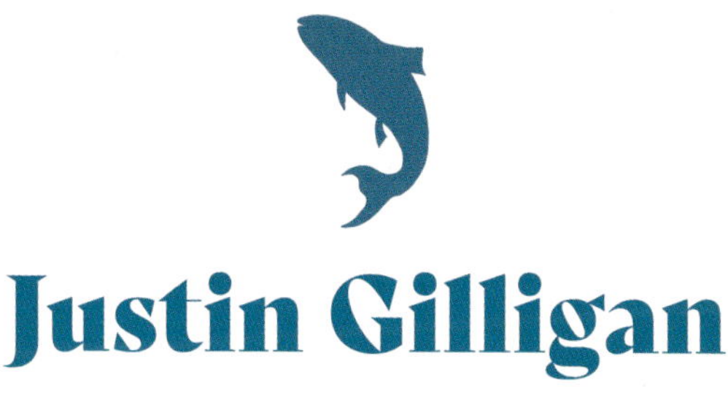

Justin Gilligan

Conservation photographer, BSc Hons

In a sense, I'm fortunate to have a perspective on Australia's marine ecosystems that can only be granted with the passing of time in the sea. With this time comes many great memories including fleeting interactions with the extraordinary and endangered.

Unfortunately, many of the changes I've witnessed have been catastrophic, and include impacts caused by coral bleaching on the Great Barrier Reef, and the reduction of giant kelp forests off Tasmania's eastern coast.

Extinction is forever. When a species is lost from an ecosystem, it can no longer play its role, incrementally decreasing ecosystem function and resilience.

As I grew up along Australia's eastern coast, I was shocked to learn how our increasing demand for seafood has resulted in declining fish stocks and bycatch; how foreshore development encroaches on sensitive coastal habitats; how run-off from cities increases marine debris; how run-off from agriculture increases nutrient pollution, and how warming seas are changing the distribution of species.

Yet, from the surface it is difficult to see these threats and impacts. Even marine scientists only get a short glimpse into the lives of their research subjects. With scuba gear, divers can only stay underwater for around an hour. It's true that we can lose a species in waters off Australia before we even know what we have lost.

The smooth handfish (*Sympterichthys unipennis*) for example, was declared extinct by the International Union for Conservation of Nature (IUCN) Red List in 2020, the first time in modern history that a marine fish species has been declared extinct. It had not been seen since it was first discovered in Tasmanian waters in 1802 by French biologist François Péron.

It's another reminder that endangered species walk an extraordinarily thin line

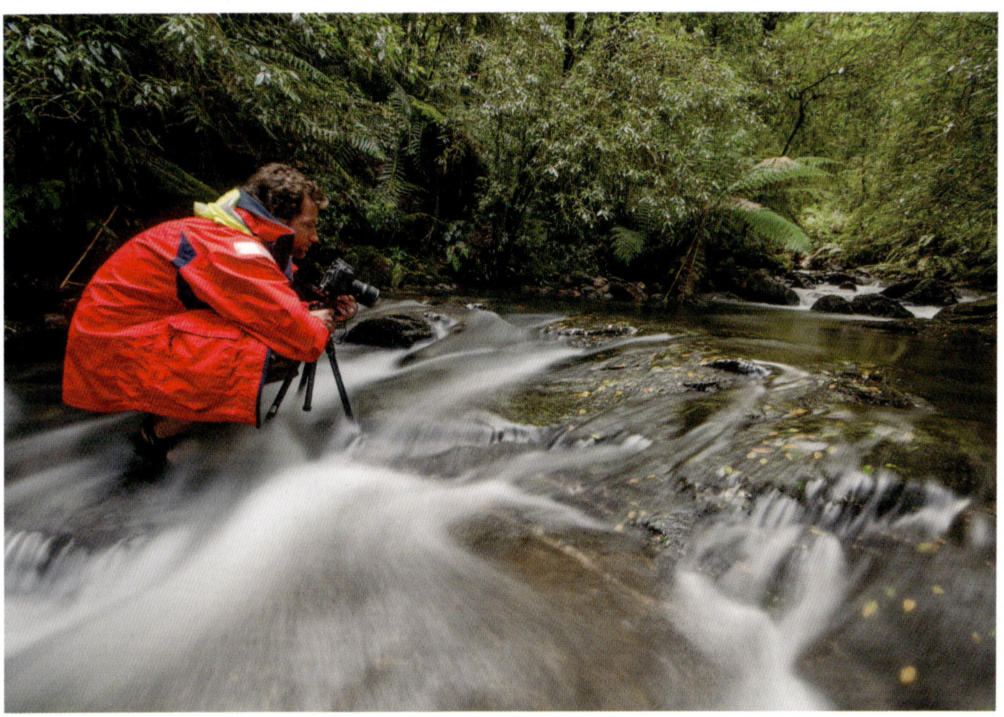

on the brink of existence. Extinction is forever. When a species is lost from an ecosystem, it can no longer play its role, incrementally decreasing ecosystem function and resilience.

But there is hope, and I have been inspired by the support of the general public and governments when the plights of our endangered species are placed in the spotlight, resulting in conservation measures that aim to correct past mistakes.

While learning to dive, and later as an experienced underwater photographer, the grey nurse shark has always been a thrilling companion, whose story provides hope and inspiration. The quintessential Aussie battler, this shark has not always been the subject of human admiration. By 1984 it was deemed on the brink of extinction – and with strong public support, it became the first shark in the world to be protected. More research followed, and soon their aggregation sites were protected as critical habitats.

Yet, the fate of many extraordinary and endangered marine species are intertwined with our strong fishing and beach culture traditions. Therefore, saving these species is a major challenge, requiring community support and ongoing research to better understand what we stand to lose.

Photograph: Glenn Gilligan.

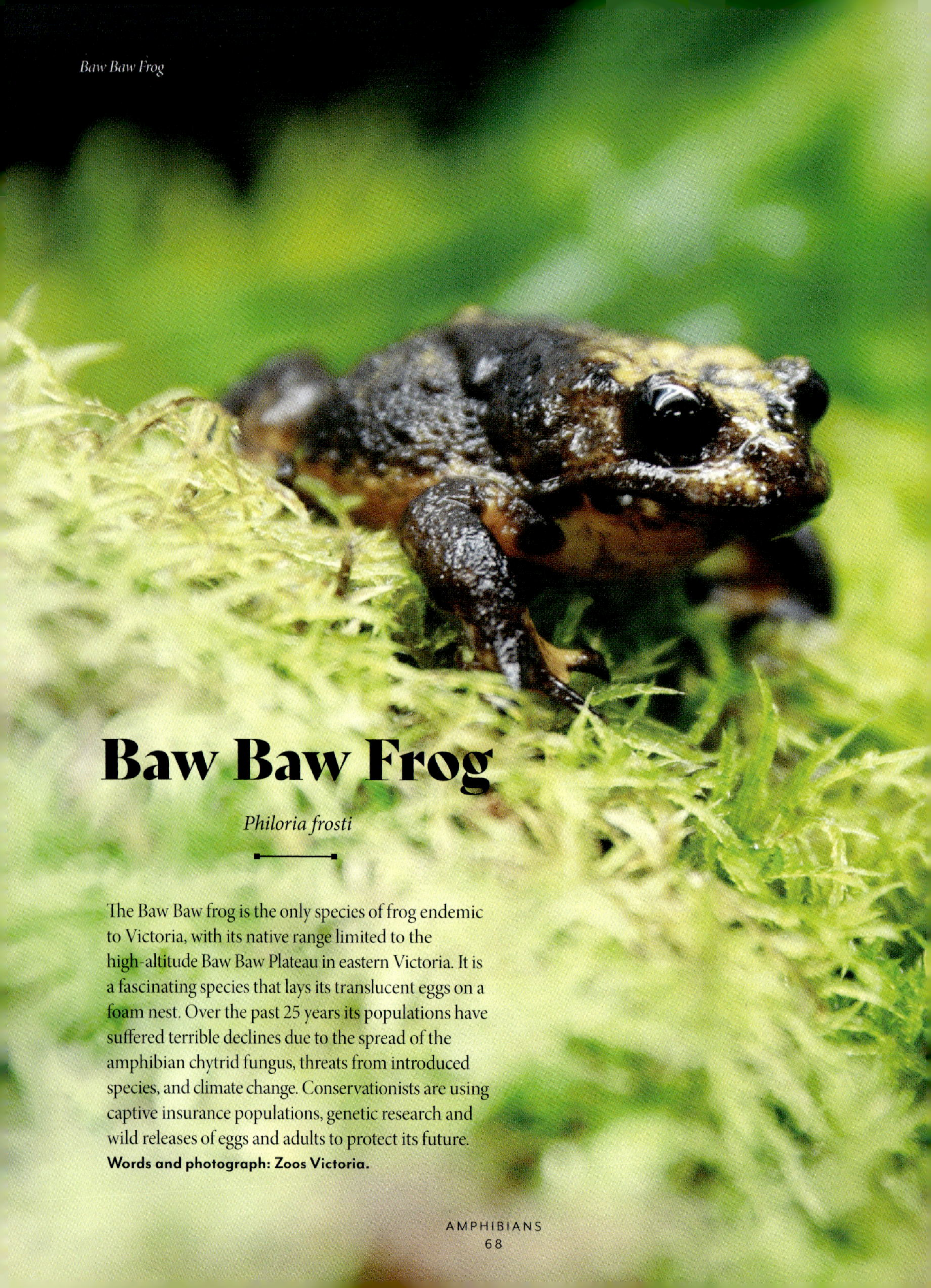

Baw Baw Frog

Philoria frosti

The Baw Baw frog is the only species of frog endemic to Victoria, with its native range limited to the high-altitude Baw Baw Plateau in eastern Victoria. It is a fascinating species that lays its translucent eggs on a foam nest. Over the past 25 years its populations have suffered terrible declines due to the spread of the amphibian chytrid fungus, threats from introduced species, and climate change. Conservationists are using captive insurance populations, genetic research and wild releases of eggs and adults to protect its future.
Words and photograph: Zoos Victoria.

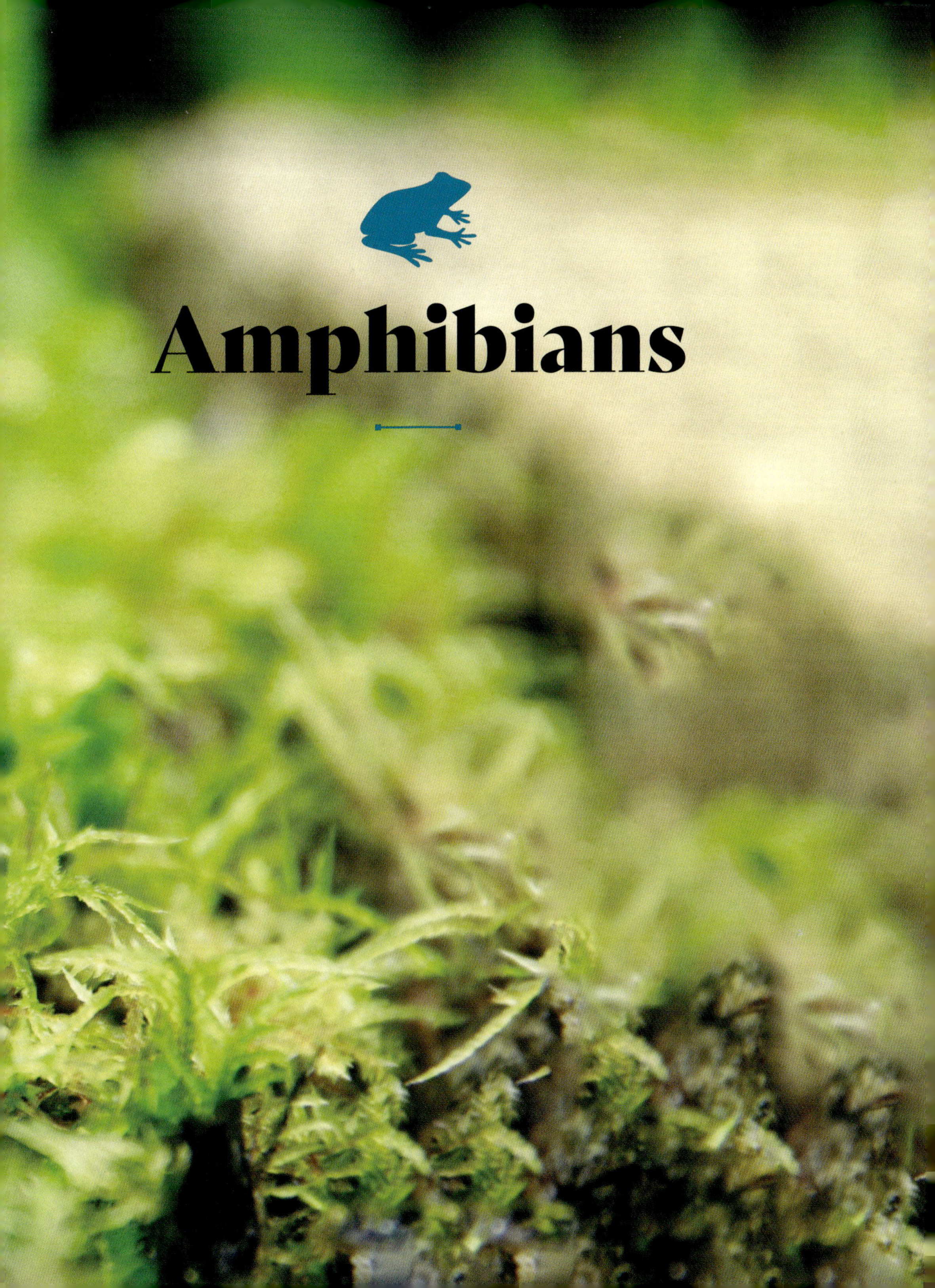

Amphibians

White-Bellied Frog

Geocrinia alba

Hidden away under leaf litter and moss within seepages in the lower south-western corner of Western Australia, male white-bellied frogs call from the nests they have created – small, damp depressions in the surrounding soil. Here, they are happy to set up shop, with genetic studies showing they rarely venture to new locations.

Their tadpoles are unique – they do not swim or feed, but rather develop entirely on land, growing completely from the large yolk supply provided by the mother. Because of this strange evolutionary quirk, the species is highly reliant on damp microhabitats to complete its life cycle. However, these are coming under increasing threat from a warming climate and increasing bushfire intensity, so the conditions these frogs need to reproduce and develop successfully are rapidly vanishing.

Words: Simon Clulow.
Photograph: Alex Cearns/Perth Zoo.

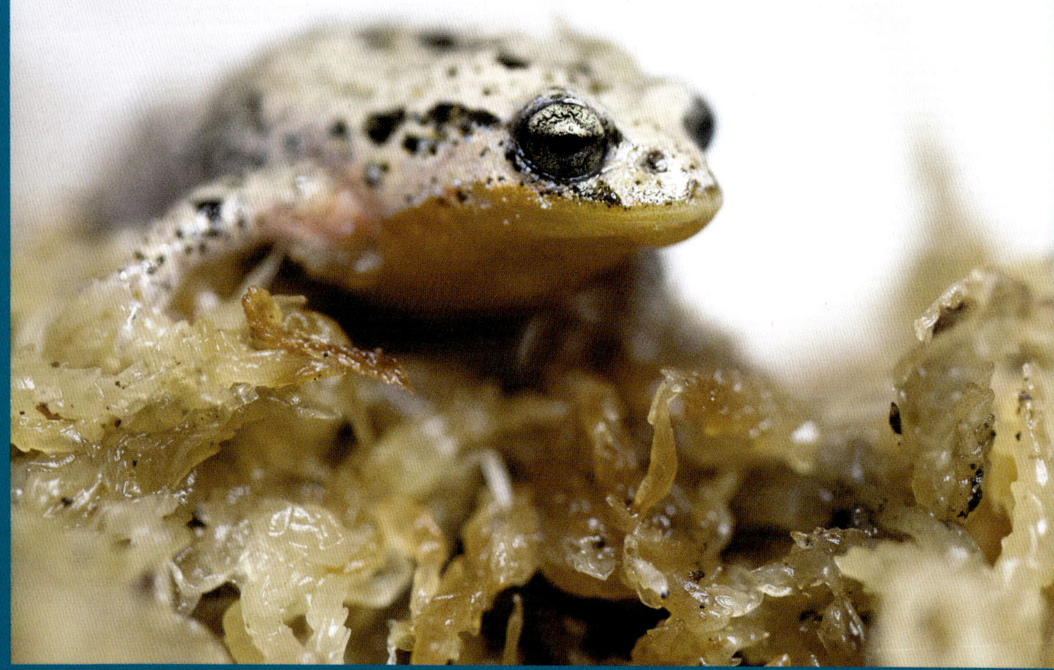

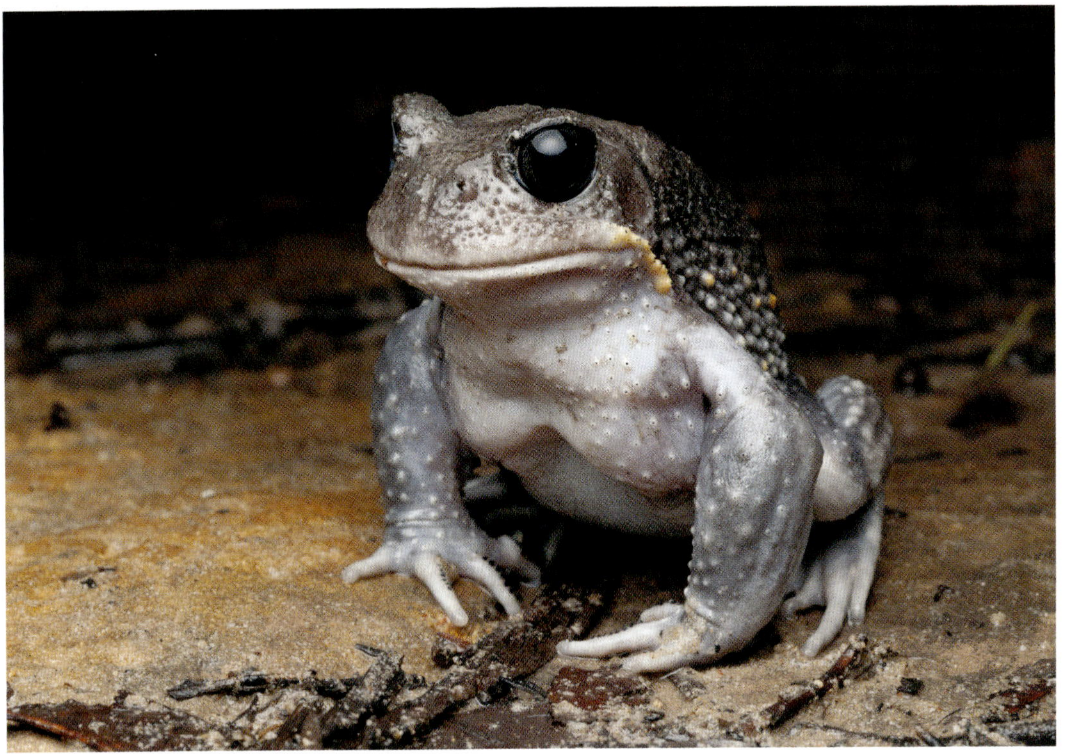

Giant Burrowing Frog

Heleioporus australiacus

As heavy rainfall soaks the sandy soils of south-eastern Australian heath and woodlands, a strange, eerie hooting noise wafts through the night air. This is quickly followed by a series of rapid-fire, owl-like 'oo-oo-oo' sounds, leaving many to ponder what sort of animal makes such a noise.

It is not a bird though, but rather the giant burrowing frog – one of the largest in Australia. Its huge, rotund frame is adorned with white or yellow spots along the flanks, and a yellow glandular ridge sits in the corner of its mouth, beneath a pair of large, bulging eyes. The males have several large nuptial spines on the first three fingers, used to clasp the female during mating and to fight rival males.

If you'd like to see a giant burrowing frog, you had best prepare for rain, as the species spends most of its time deep under the sand. It even lays its frothy egg masses in moist burrows under the banks of small creeks.

Words: Simon Clulow.
Photograph: Stephen Mahony.

Green And Golden Bell Frog

Litoria aurea

Patterned in striking bronze, green and gold, male green and golden bell frogs gather in groups among wetland reeds, ready to call in loud choruses. Their calls are distinct, filling the air with sounds similar to a motorbike revving as it changes gears. If disturbed, the frogs leap into the safety of the water, revealing a dazzling bright turquoise blue in the groin area that remains mostly hidden while perched.

This frog was once so common in eastern Australia's wetlands that it was regularly collected by universities and used in animal dissections. Now, it occurs in only around 10 per cent of its former range, restricted to isolated coastal pockets.

Words: Simon Clulow.
Photograph: Alex Pike/DPIE.

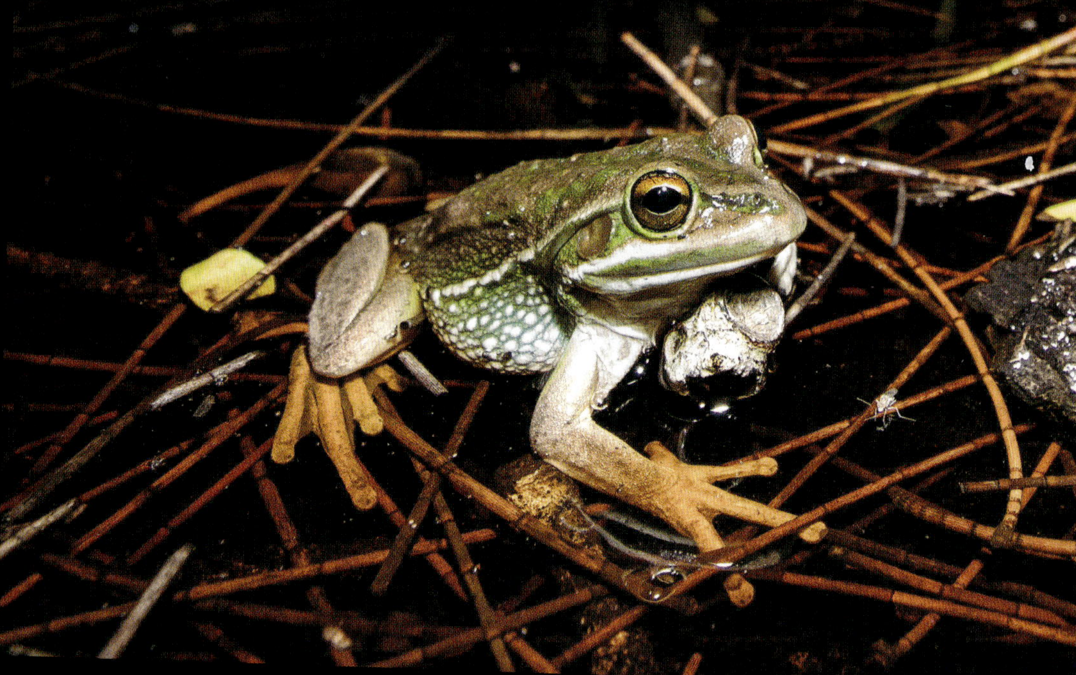

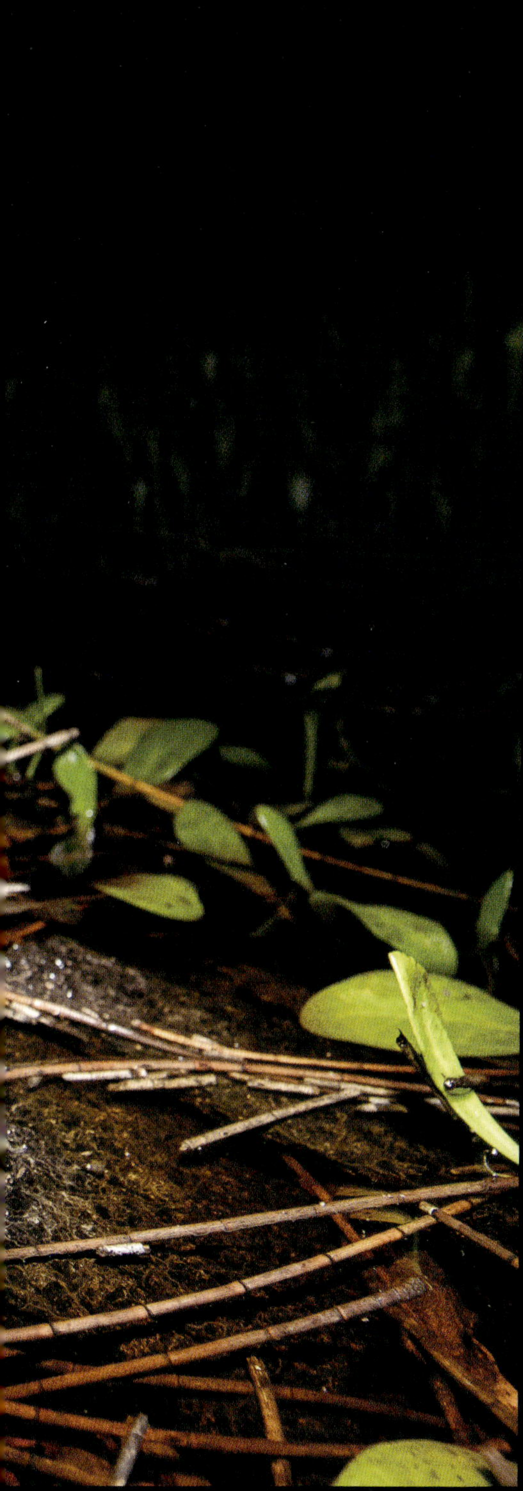

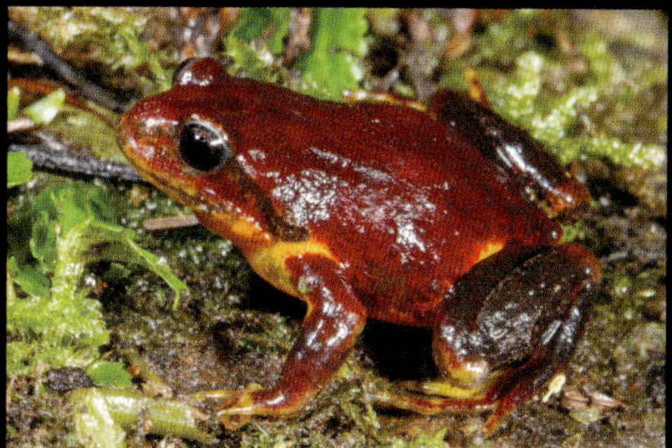

Mountain Frog

Philoria kundagungan

In a tiny area from the Mistake Mountains in south-eastern Queensland to the Beaury State Forest just across the border of NSW, a small, secretive frog lies hidden away, nesting in bogs beneath rocks and leaves in small, soaked holes. Only a slow, guttural 'bork' gives away its location – a pity, because it is quite a sight to see. Its colour ranges from spectacular shades of bright reds, yellows, oranges and purple-red to red-brown. At its most spectacular, it can look like it has received a healthy coating of tomato sauce. Even its belly is a bright yellow colour.

Somewhat unusually for a frog, it can often be heard calling during the day. The tadpoles are as unlikely to be found as the adults – females deposit their eggs in foamy masses within the nests, beaten to a froth by paddle-like structures on their first and second fingers. The tadpoles rarely leave the nests, feeding on their own yolk reserves and remaining in the broken-down egg mass.

Words: Simon Clulow. Photograph: Stephen Zozaya.

Hip-Pocket Frog

Assa darlingtoni

From the rainforest floors of northern NSW and south-eastern Queensland, a frog the size of a human thumbnail calls for mates from deep within the leaf litter. Here, males engage in games rarely observed in the animal kingdom – sustained bouts of attempting to synchronise their rapidly repeating, machine gun-like calls. Whether this is a form of cooperation to confuse predators, or competition to drown out their neighbours, remains unknown.

But its strangest behaviour of all relates to its unique reproductive mode. Male hip-pocket frogs have a pair of small, outwardly opening brood pouches near their groin. Here, the tadpoles wriggle inside, and the males carry them around in their 'hip-pockets' until they complete metamorphosis. The young then emerge as fully functioning froglets, about the size of a match-head. It amounts to one of the most unique forms of parental care among the animal kingdom, and is a rare example of male parental care in frogs.

Words: Simon Clulow.
Photograph: Stephen Mahony.

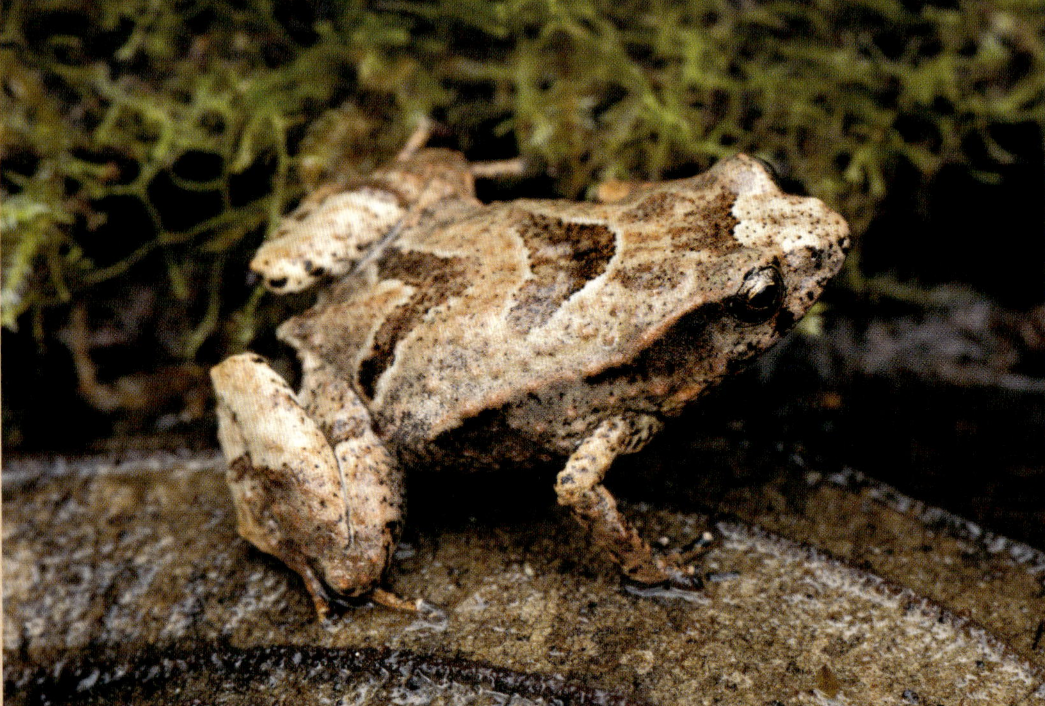

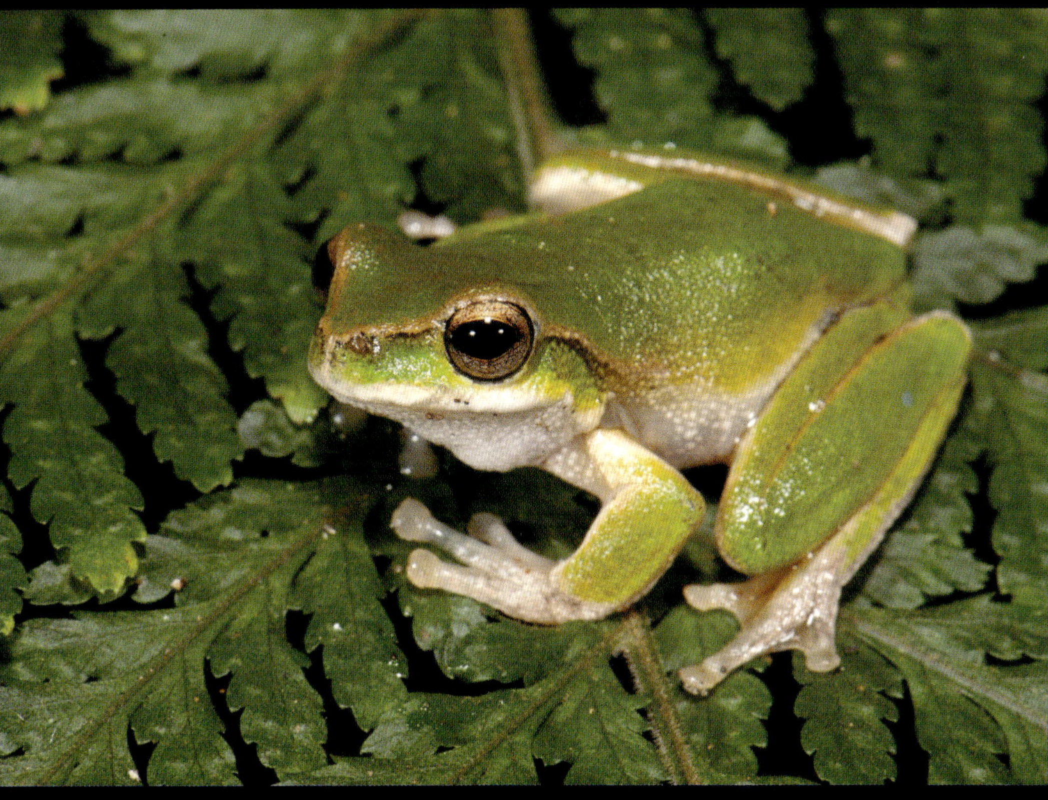

Kroombit Tree Frog

Litoria kroombitensis

Along flowing streams of the rainforest and wet sclerophyll forest of the Kroombit Tops, a small frog chatters away from the ferns and overhanging branches that line the creeks. This is the Kroombit Tops's very own frog, found nowhere else on earth.

The frog is saturated in deep leaf-green, blending into the chlorophyll-soaked leaves it clings to. The green on the back and head is broken only by a thin, gold line down the middle of the face, bordered by another thin black line below it, appearing almost to be painted like an intricate Fabergé egg.

Unfortunately, the Kroombit tree frog is thought to be badly impacted by a disease caused by an amphibian-killing fungus that has spread throughout Australia, and it is now facing an uncertain future.

Words: Simon Clulow.
Photograph: Angus McNab.

Southern Corroboree Frog

Pseudophryne corroboree

In the soaks and sphagnum bogs of the snow-capped mountaintops of Kosciuszko National Park, a small jewel is hidden away. Remaining silent during the winter months, when it can be buried beneath snow and ice, the only thing that gives this jewel away from its hiding spot is a soft squelch-like call when it warms up enough to signal for mates in the summer. Uncover it from its hiding spot and you'll be greeted by a brilliant display of black and yellow stripes adorning the entire body – often likened to ceremonial paint in preparation for a corroboree. These striking markings serve a purpose – they warn would-be predators that these frogs are poisonous.

Unfortunately, the Critically Endangered southern corroboree frog is one of Australia's most threatened amphibians, with only about 50 left in the wild.

Words: Simon Clulow.
Photograph: Zoos Victoria.

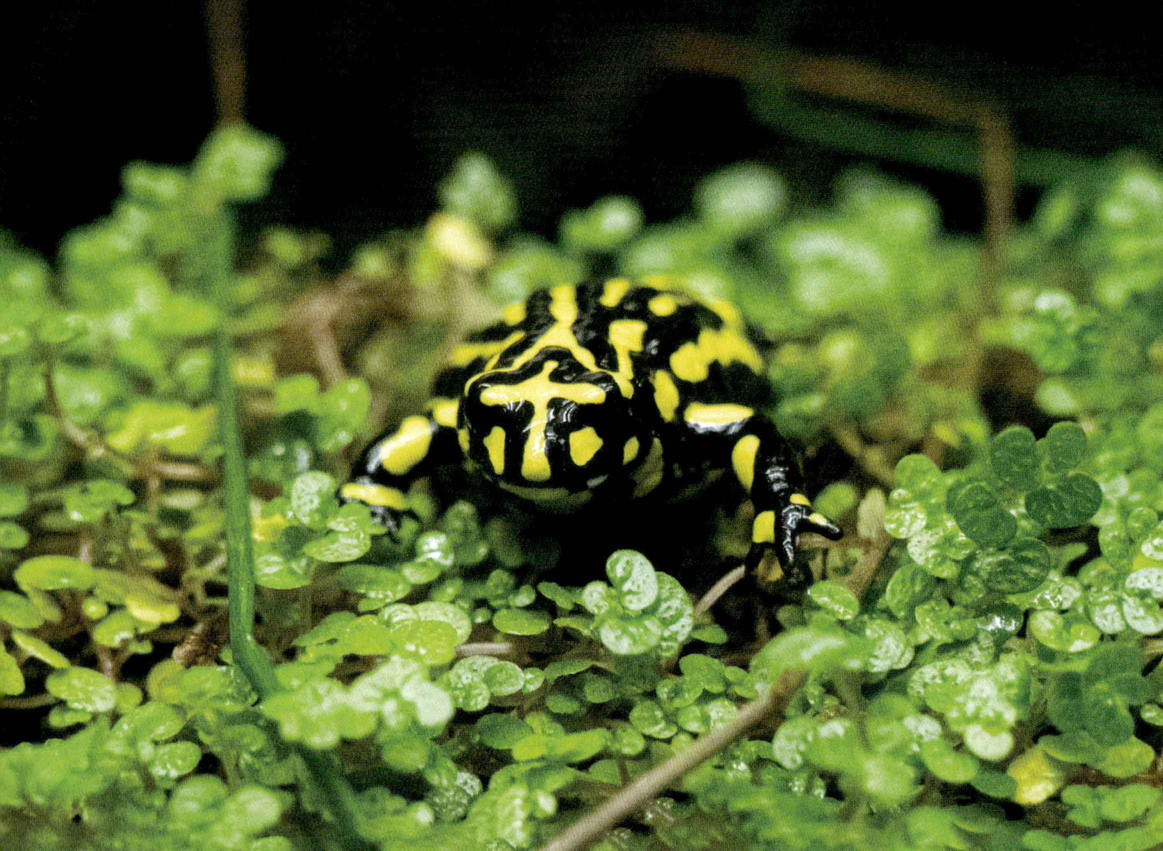

Kuranda Tree Frog

Litoria myola

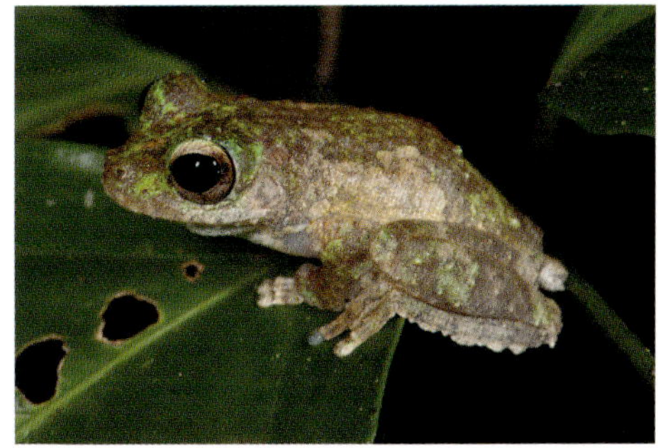

Along the streams of a small patch of rainforest near Kuranda in northern Queensland there lives a frog with piercing eyes. As if ready for a night on the town, the Kuranda tree frog has an iridescent green upper margin to its iris, like a thin band of eyeshadow. The rest of the iris is a deep silver-gold with dark reticulations and veins throughout, which makes it difficult to resist staring deeply into the eyes of this stunning little frog.

Its body form is also interesting – the outer edges of the forearms and feet are lined with serrated fringes, presumably for blending into its background. On the heel is a small, pointed cone-shaped lappet, also unique to the species. Its back has patches of moss-green over orange and chocolate-brown, matching its distinct eyeshadow.

Known only from a tiny patch near Myola, the Critically Endangered Kuranda tree frog is severely threatened by the amphibian-killing chytrid fungus and habitat loss, and there is worry over its future.

Words: Simon Clulow.
Photograph: Stephen Mahony.

Southern Gastric-Brooding Frog

Rheobatrachus silus

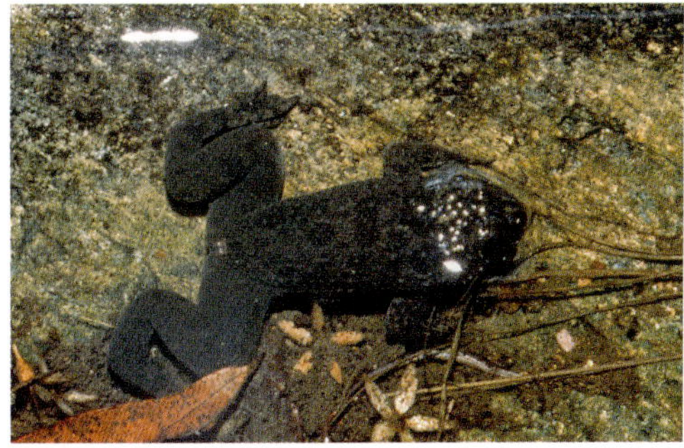

In rainforest streams of the Conondale Ranges of south-eastern Queensland, the southern gastric-brooding frog is well adapted to life in water. It is one of just two species of aquatic frog native to Australia, with upwardly projecting eyes, and skin coated in a heavy mucous that makes it slippery to catch. But its most remarkable feature is its reproductive cycle. The females temporarily convert their stomach into a makeshift womb by switching off gastric secretions and stopping contractions involved with feeding. They then rear their young within their stomach until they metamorphose. At this point, the female gives birth to fully-formed frogs from its mouth, a reproductive mode not only unique among amphibians, but among all animals on earth.

Unfortunately, the southern gastric-brooding frog – along with its close sister species, the northern gastric-brooding frog – is believed to be extinct, so we may have lost one of evolution's most remarkable solutions for ensuring reproductive success.

Words: Simon Clulow. Photograph: Steve Wilson.

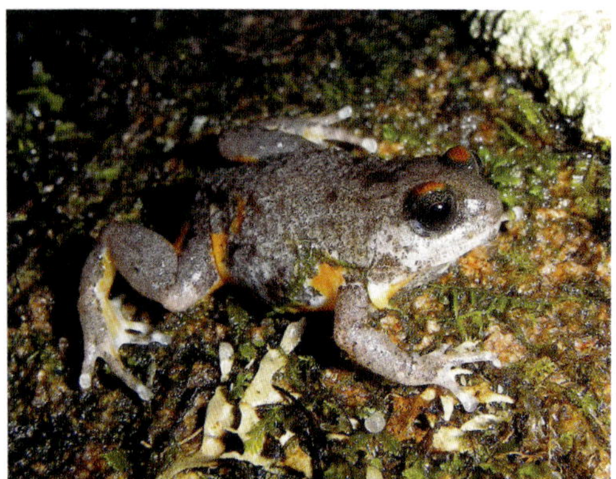

Elegant Frog

Cophixalus concinnus

Perched on shrubs and ferns above the rainforest floor, sometimes with a distinct red patch on the back of each eye, male elegant frogs let out a short trill lasting little more than a second. They are calling to attract mates to their nests, which are situated about two metres off the forest floor. Here, the female deposits a small number of large, yolky eggs in a linked rosary chain. Rather than hatch into water and become free-swimming tadpoles like many frogs, the embryos survive completely off the large yolk reserves supplied by the mother and they complete metamorphosis entirely within the egg, eventually hatching as fully formed frogs.

The elegant frog exists entirely within rainforest and boulder fields of the Thornton Peak Uplands in Far North Queensland, above elevations of 1100m.

Words: Simon Clulow. Photograph: Steve Williams.

Armoured Mist Frog

Litoria lorica

Deep in northern Queensland, fast-flowing rainforest streams strewn with boulders roar to life with each new rainfall. This is prime habitat for mist frogs – named for the mist that fills the air in their habitat, churned up by waterfalls and rapids.

Heavily marbled to blend in with the surrounding granite, armoured mist frogs dance around boulders within the fast-flowing streams. They are superb swimmers, and are thought to attach their eggs in clumps to the rocks to avoid them being washed away.

The males contain conspicuous small black spines along the inner finger, upper lip and chest, likely for holding onto females during breeding. The tadpoles are well adapted to living in moving water, with long, slender bodies, and mouth-parts like sucker pads that hold on to rocks so they are not washed away.

Words: Simon Clulow.
Photograph: Dr Robert Puschendorf.

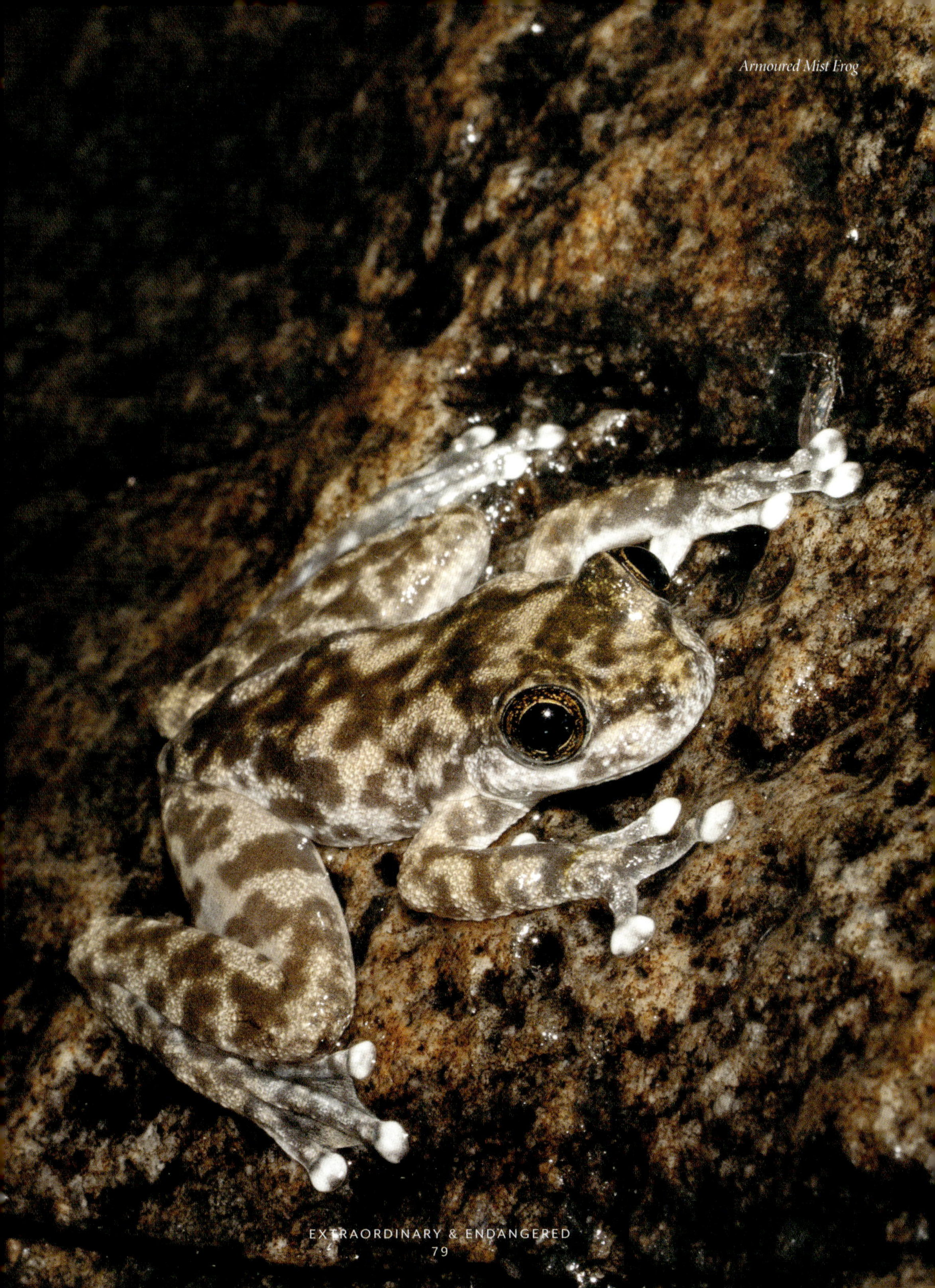
Armoured Mist Frog

Red-Crowned Toadlet

Pseudophryne australis

Along seepages and drainage lines atop sandstone escarpments across the Sydney Basin, a short, clicky squelch can be heard emanating from beneath the dry eucalyptus leaf litter. It's the call of the red-crowned toadlet, which constructs its nests in the moist bogs and soils lining these soaks.

So named for the bright red crown that adorns its head, the red-crowned toadlet deposits its eggs in these nests. Here, the tadpoles undergo development to an advanced hatching stage, before entering embryonic diapause, waiting for it to rain. When the rain finally comes, the water triggers hatching, and the tadpoles get washed down into pools where they can complete metamorphosis. This spectacular amphibian is restricted entirely to the Hawkesbury sandstone of the Sydney Basin.

Words: Simon Clulow.
Photograph: Stephen Mahony.

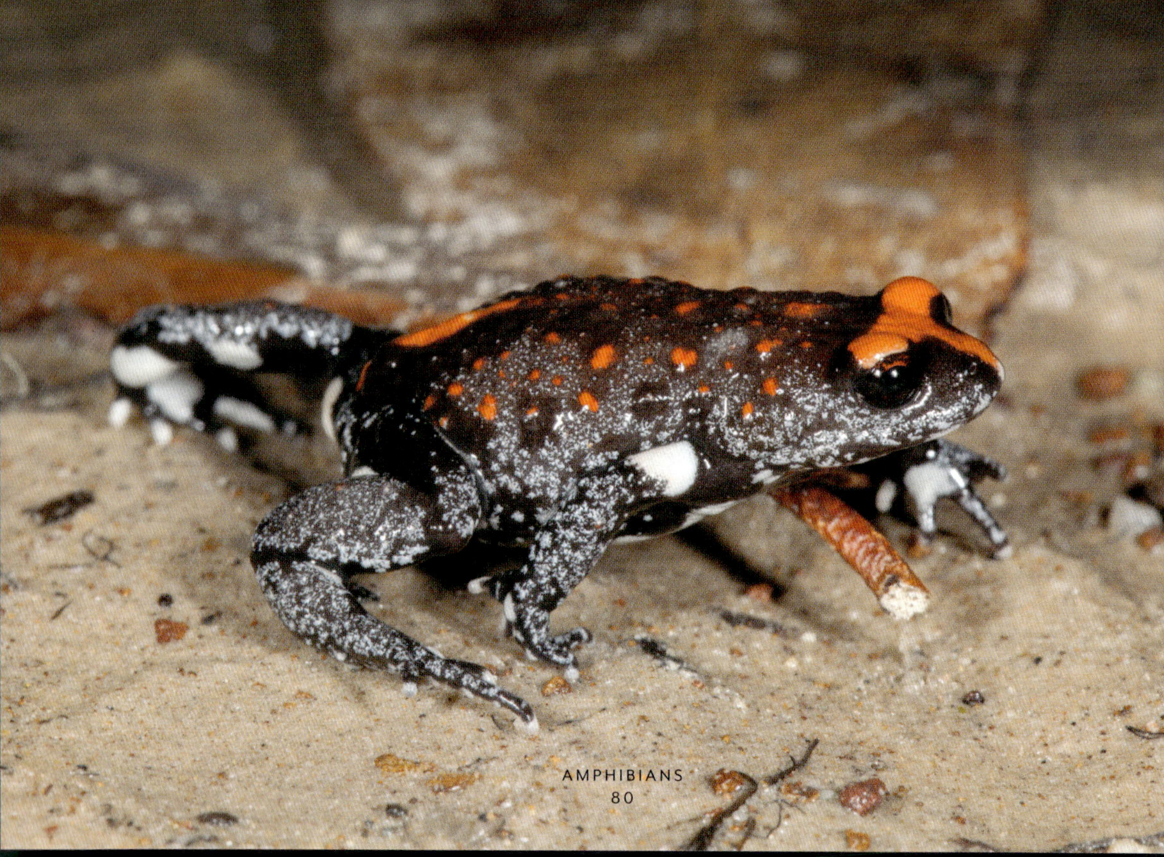

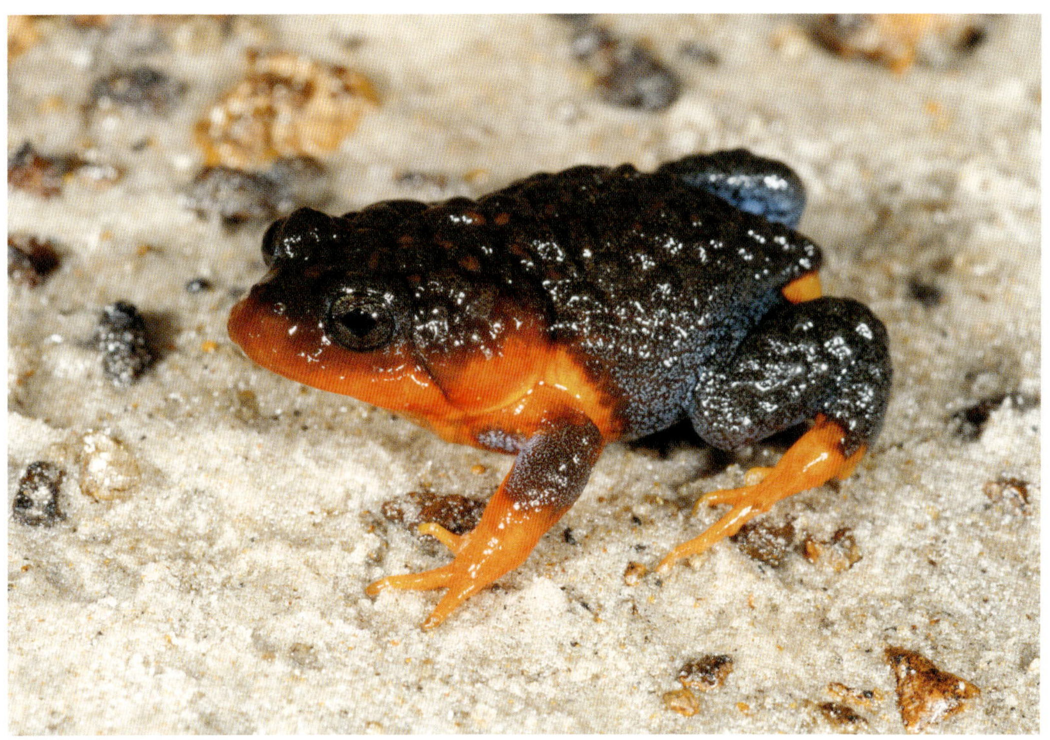

Sunset Frog

Spicospina flammocaerulea

Restricted to a small area around Walpole in south-western Western Australia, the sunset frog is one of Australia's most restricted and striking frogs, measuring around 3.5cm. A bright orange-yellow band runs around its snout and down onto its arms, reminiscent of a marvellous sunset or a spectacular lava flow. Its hands and feet also look like they've been dipped in molten lava, bearing the same brilliant colours of steel about to melt. But it is perhaps its belly that is most striking, with vivid patches of blue on a blackish background that meet the bright orange-yellow of the throat.

Listed as Vulnerable, sunset frogs are also unique in the habitat they occupy. They lay their eggs in highly acidic, peaty swamps that few other frogs inhabit.

Words: Simon Clulow. Photograph: Mark Sanders/EcoSmart Ecology.

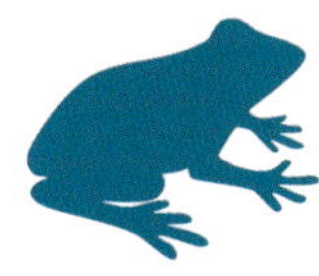

Deon Gilbert

Zoos Victoria Threatened Species Biologist

I've been working with Threatened frogs all of my adult life, but in truth the fascination began much earlier. When people ask me when I first became interested in frogs, I honestly don't have an answer for them. I can't remember.

I was fortunate enough to grow up surrounded by the bush and wildlife, and as a child I think that fostered a subconscious love for the natural world that has stayed with me.

Frogs show me that no matter how seemingly insignificant you might be, you have a role to play.

Frogs have always been so mysterious to me, and continue to be the focus of that fascination. Perhaps it's because they begin life in the water as eggs and tadpoles, then completely transform, as if by magic, and move onto land as frogs. Or maybe it's that when I close my eyes and imagine the Australian soundscape, I hear a frog chorus along with a kookaburra's laugh, and the wind in the eucalyptus trees. Or perhaps they show me how interconnected everything is for our global health, from prey to predator to ecosystem function.

Frogs show me that no matter how seemingly insignificant you might be, you have a role to play. Tadpole or frog, lion or gorilla, you or me – we are all intrinsically linked, and what we do to one eventually affects the other. Asking why something matters seems like such a backwards question. We're in the midst of a mass extinction and catastrophic environmental change – all because we keep asking why we should care if something goes extinct, or why something matters.

When you finish reading this book, go into nature and just sit, close your eyes and listen; be conscious of your place in it. Just like the tadpole or frog, you have a role to play. Don't ask yourself why something matters; ask yourself what you can to do ensure it does.

Photograph: Zoos Victoria.

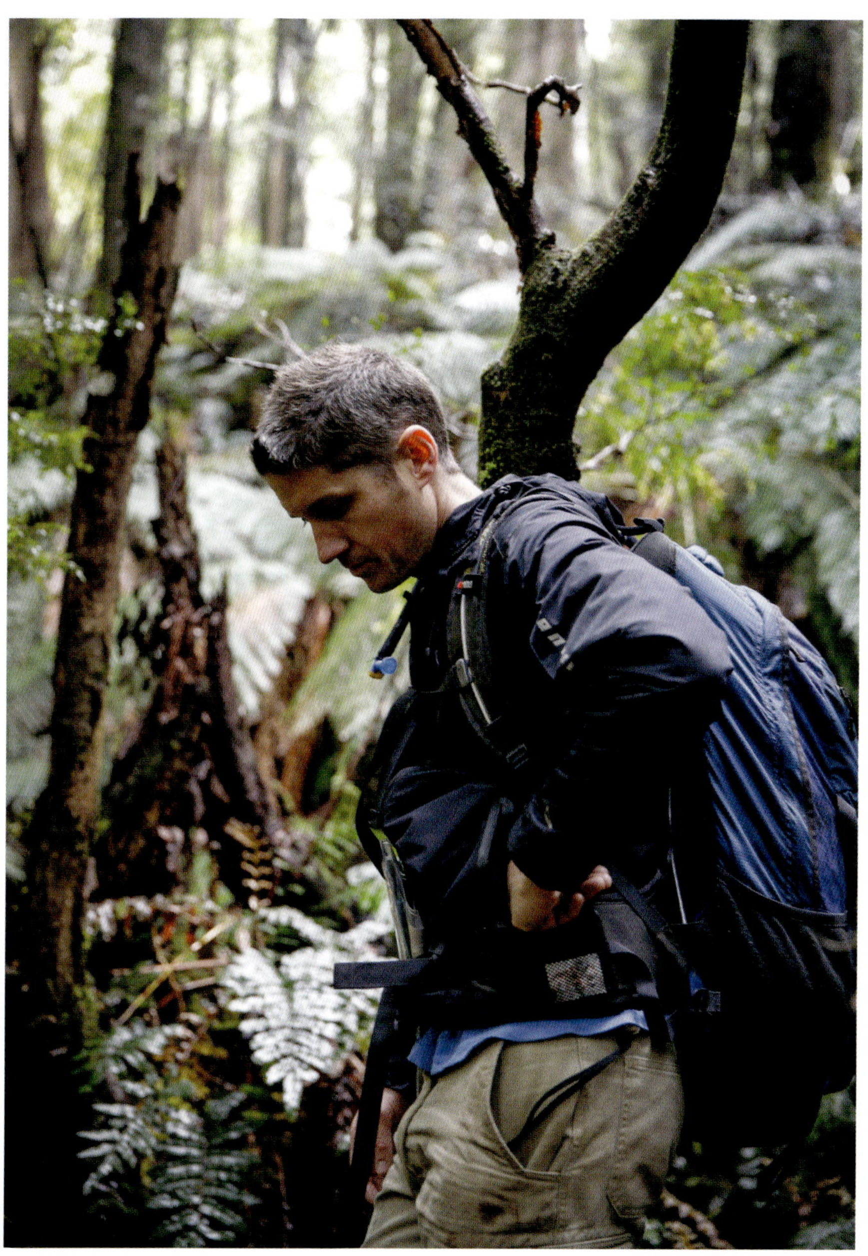

Key's Matchstick Grasshopper

This grasshopper was once found throughout the extensive grasslands of southern New South Wales and Victoria. Since colonisation, these habitats have largely disappeared, but remnants can be found in cemeteries, travelling cattle stock reserves, and some natural areas.

Like a ghost of the past landscape, Key's matchstick grasshopper can be found amongst the kangaroo grass of these areas. The patchiness of these habitats threatens the future of this grasshopper however, as their wingless form limits their ability to travel long distances. Poor management of these areas has led to further declines of the grasshopper's populations, but conservation efforts are focused on improving the management of its existing habitats and understanding the mysterious ecology of this endemic insect.

Words: Jessa Thurman.
Photograph: Dr Michael Kearney.

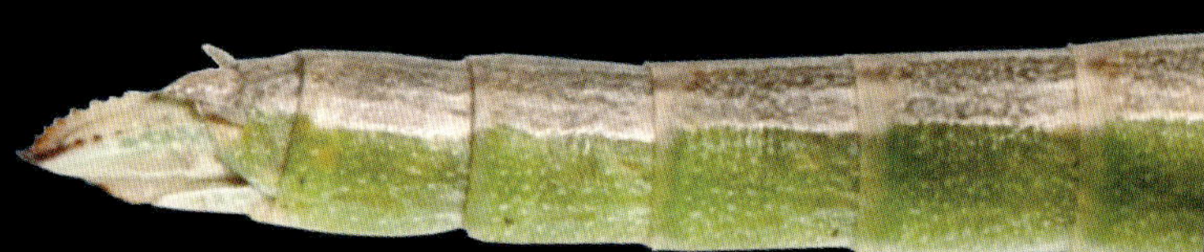

Invertebrates

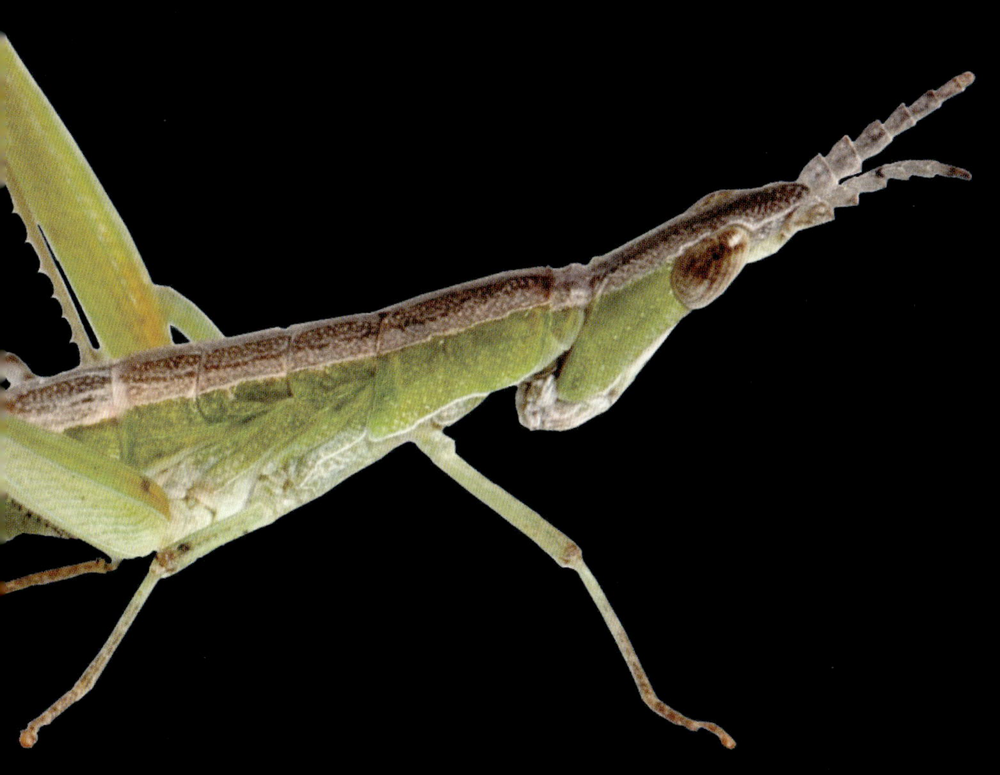

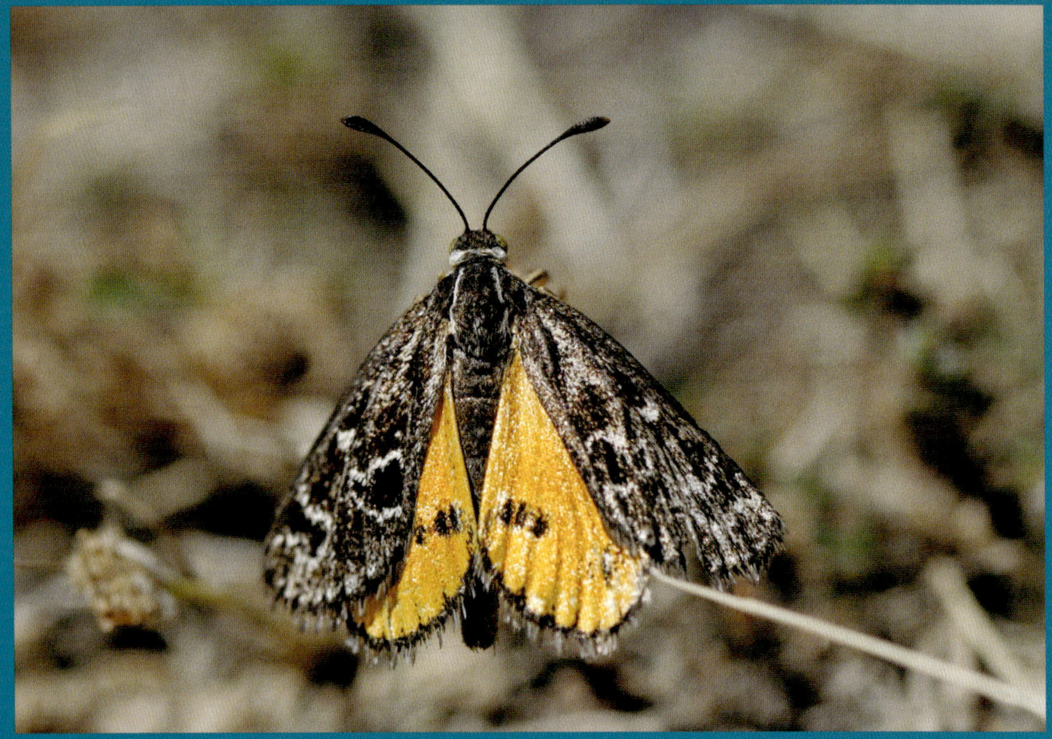

Golden Sun Moth

Synemon plana

This moth behaves like and resembles a butterfly, flying during the warmest parts of the day and having clubbed antennae. Their forewings are brown and help them blend in with their grassland homes, but the underwings of females are bright gold. The females rest in the grass and display their golden wings to attract passing males.

The caterpillars of this species feed underground on the rhizomes of wallaby grass (*Austrodanthonia spp.*), but the grassland habitats where these are most common are Critically Endangered. Farming has destroyed much of the native grasslands in the Bathurst region of NSW down to the border of Victoria and South Australia where this moth is found, limiting the insect to a few remnant patches.

Words: Jessa Thurman.
Photograph: Leo Berzins.

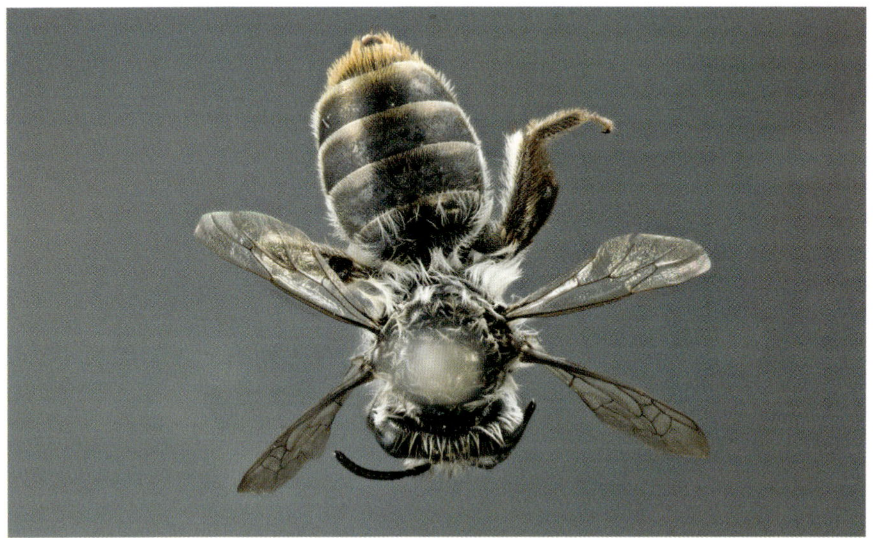

Douglas' Broad-Headed Bee; Rottnest Bee

Hesperocolletes douglasi

The Douglas' broad-headed bee was first collected on Rottnest Island, Western Australia, in 1938. Then it wasn't seen again for 80 years, and was presumed extinct, with extensive surveys unable to locate it. Nothing was known about this bee, yet it seemed lost. That is, until 2015, when it was collected as part of a survey of pollinators in the remnant banksia woodlands surrounding Perth. This survey collected the first female of this unique species, and analysed the pollen that it was carrying to determine what plants it relies on.

This discovery emphasises the importance of habitat conservation for preserving rare and threatened species. We have been given a second chance with the Douglas' broad-headed bee – we cannot fail it now.

Words: Jessa Thurman.
Photograph: Dr Juliana Pille Arnold

Southern Pink Underwing Moth

Phyllodes imperialis smithersi

This moth spends its life pretending to be things that it is not. Wings of adult moths resemble dead leaves and even have silver markings that look like leaf-mines left by other insects. If a predator is not fooled by these false-leaves, the moth can flash the bright pink spots on its hindwings to startle the predator, and escape. The caterpillars of this moth can also resemble a snake by curling their heads to emphasise two large eyespots on their body.

Despite these special adaptations, the moth is no match for habitat loss, and it is currently Endangered due to the reduction of rainforests in south-eastern Queensland and northern NSW.

Words and photograph: Jessa Thurman.

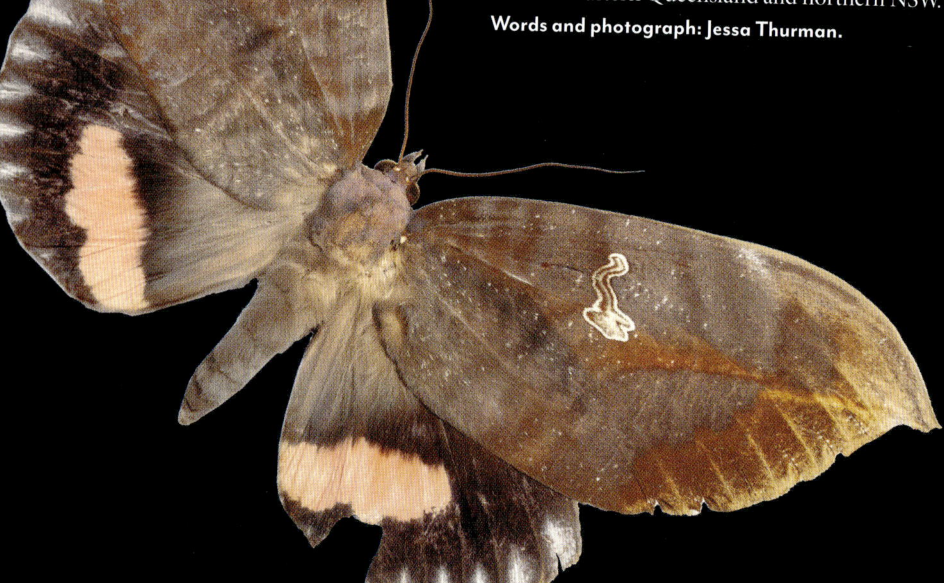

Kangaroo Island Pelican Spider

Zephyrarchaea austini

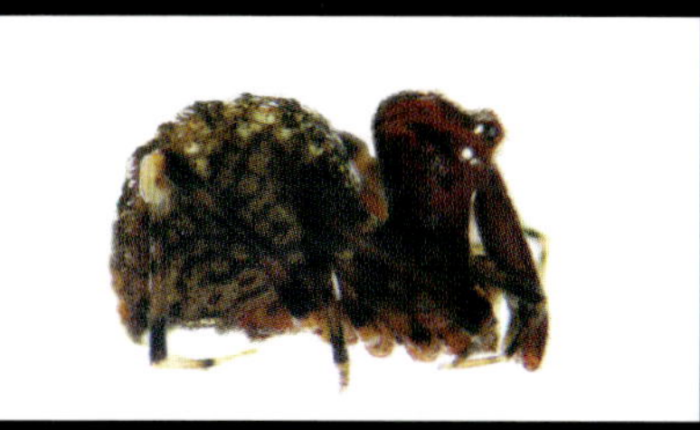

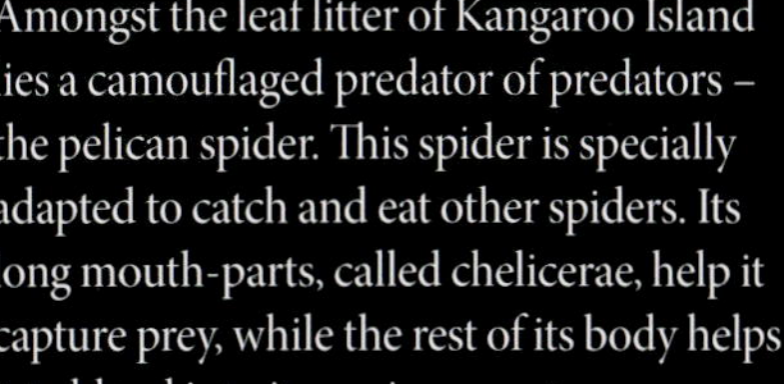

Amongst the leaf litter of Kangaroo Island lies a camouflaged predator of predators – the pelican spider. This spider is specially adapted to catch and eat other spiders. Its long mouth-parts, called chelicerae, help it capture prey, while the rest of its body helps it to blend into its environment.

This particular species is part of an ancient group of spiders that hasn't changed much over the past 150 million years. Now, however, this species is under threat from climate change. Devastating bushfires in 2020 on Kangaroo Island destroyed all of its known habitat, but recent surveys have found two individuals in a small remnant patch of habitat.

Words: Jessa Thurman.
Photograph: Dr Jessica Marsh.

Giant Gippsland Earthworm

Megascolides australis

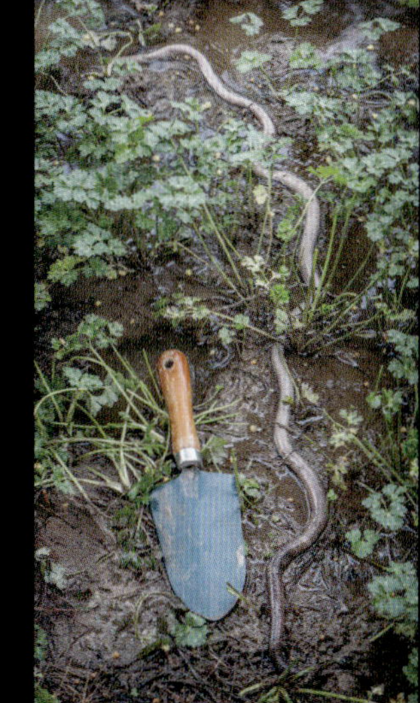

The giant Gippsland earthworm can be heard squelching through its large underground burrows in the wet clay soils of the Gippsland region in Victoria. It is one of the largest known earthworms in the world, with records showing it can grow to over a metre long (and old reports of them being up to 3m). They can change their length and width as they move, which makes confirming their exact measurements difficult.

This species is long-lived, and each individual can produce only one egg case per year. These earthworms are also limited to patches of suitable habitat with well-draining soils – habitats that have been largely cleared for farming, resulting in erosion. The worms are also vulnerable to flooding and drying events, which can become more frequent with climate change.

Conservation efforts have been focused on locating known colonies of worms, protecting these places, and learning more about the ecology of this hidden giant to protect it into the future.

Words: Jessa Thurman. Photograph: Dr Beverley Van Praagh.

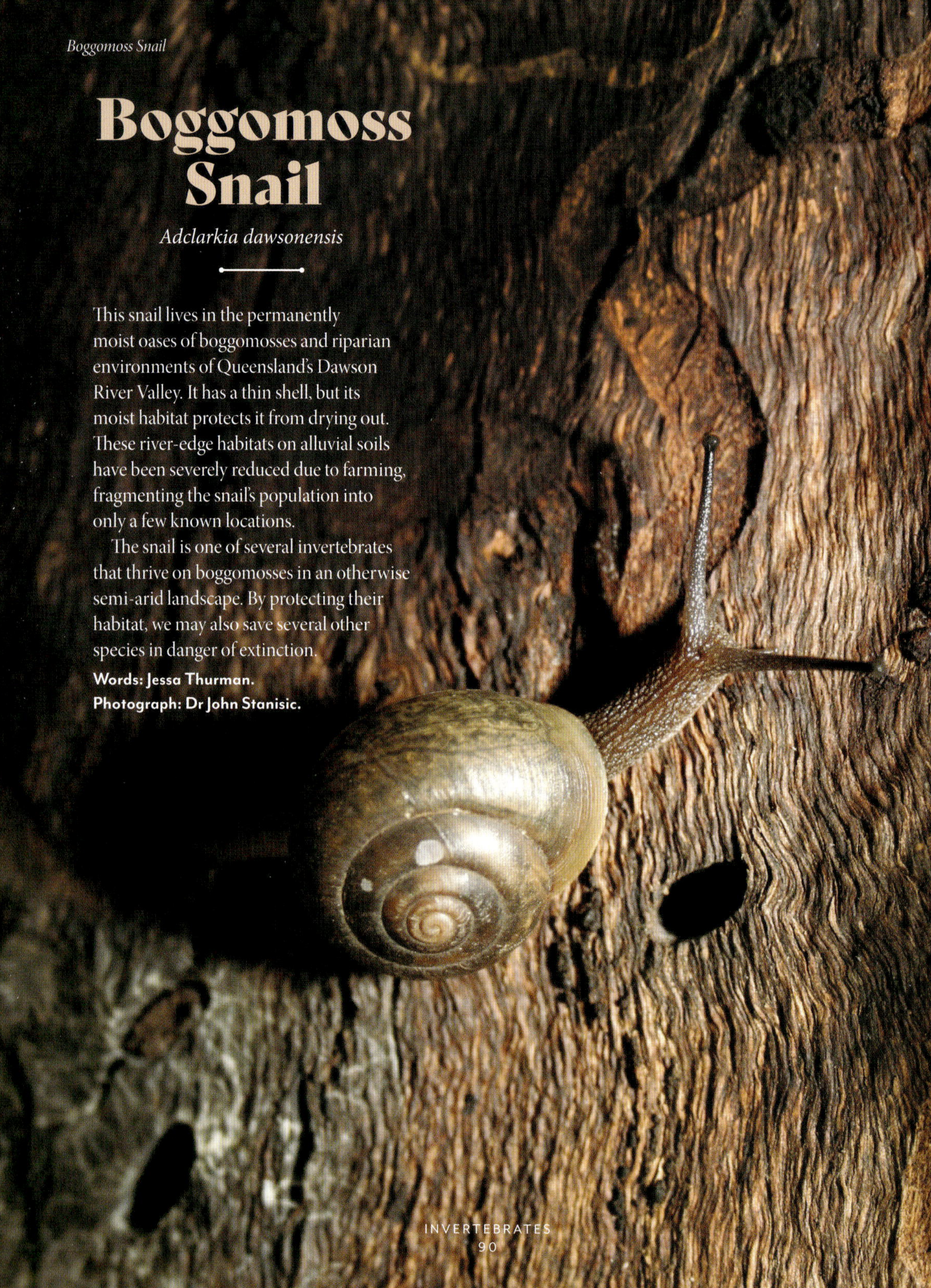

Boggomoss Snail

Adclarkia dawsonensis

This snail lives in the permanently moist oases of boggomosses and riparian environments of Queensland's Dawson River Valley. It has a thin shell, but its moist habitat protects it from drying out. These river-edge habitats on alluvial soils have been severely reduced due to farming, fragmenting the snail's population into only a few known locations.

The snail is one of several invertebrates that thrive on boggomosses in an otherwise semi-arid landscape. By protecting their habitat, we may also save several other species in danger of extinction.

Words: Jessa Thurman.
Photograph: Dr John Stanisic.

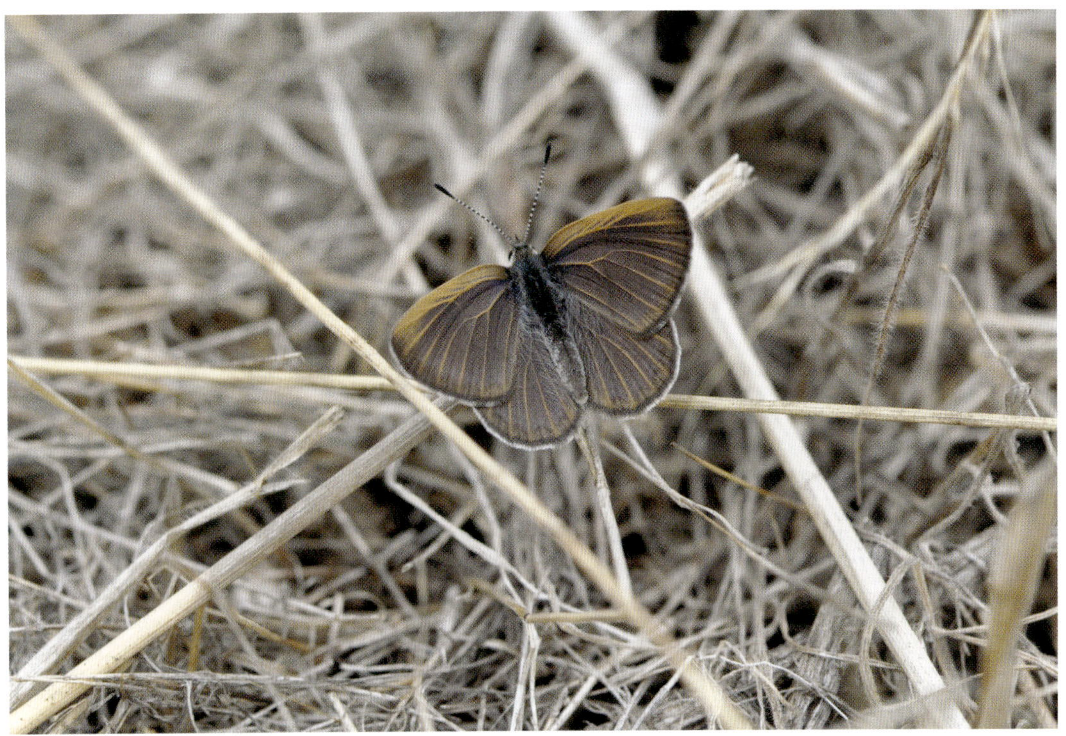

Golden-Rayed Blue Butterfly

Candalides noelkeri

The golden-rayed blue butterfly can be seen basking in the sun. Males of this species vary in colour, with purple, pinkish purple, or even bronze wings. Females lay their eggs one by one on the flower buds of a ground cover plant called creeping boobialla (*Myoporum parvifolium*), which grows along saline floodplains bordering natural salt lakes in western Victoria.

While the butterfly can be found commonly in these areas, the habitat for this butterfly and its plant are being degraded by paperbarks (*Melaleuca halmaturorum*). Weed management and habitat protection will ensure the future of this critically endangered butterfly.

Words: Jessa Thurman. Photograph: Kate Pearce/Zoos Victoria.

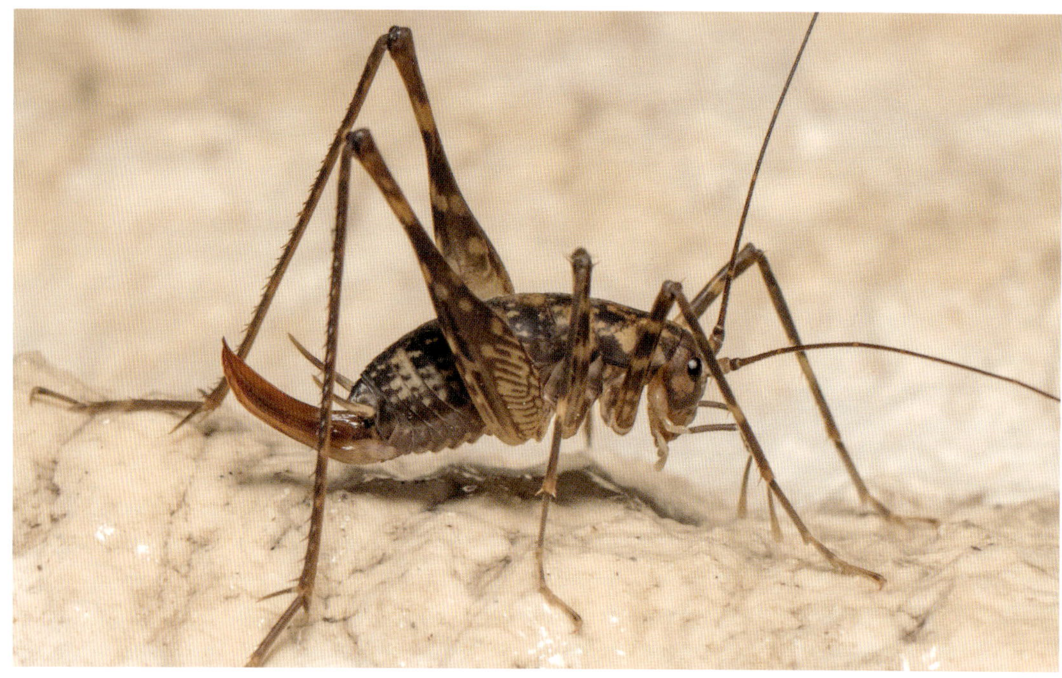

Francistown or Southern Sandstone Cave Cricket

Micropathus kiernani

Colonies of sandstone cave crickets dwell in the moist crevices of Tasmania's caves and mines. While these crickets spend most of their lives underground, some species are suspected to forage in the forest habitats that surround their cave entrances.

The southern sandstone cave cricket has the most restricted distribution of its kind, and has only been found in caves of south-eastern Tasmania near Francistown.

The forests which surround these caves may play a key role in the cricket's survival, as they could supply food resources and help maintain the microclimate of the caves.

Little is known about this cricket's ecology, however, and research must be done to understand how we can help spare it from extinction.

Words: Jessa Thurman. Photograph of *Micropathus* species: Tim Rudman.

Bornemissza's Stag Beetle

Hoplogonus bornemisszai

Buried in the leaf litter of north-eastern Tasmania's wet forests is the Bornemissza's stag beetle – a species suspected to live for four years, spending half of its life as a larva that feeds on decomposing matter in the soil. Adult males can be found in early summer when they're thought to seek out females to mate with.

The wet forests where this species lives are under threat from habitat loss and degradation. Healthy forests appear to be key to this species' survival as it relies on deep layers of accumulated leaf litter. This species is only found in a limited area near St Helens, Tasmania, and cannot fly, suggesting that a loss of this habitat would eliminate the species. By studying the ecology of this beetle and protecting the small amount of habitat it has left, we can ensure it will continue to thrive.

Words: Jessa Thurman.
Photograph: Dash Huang.

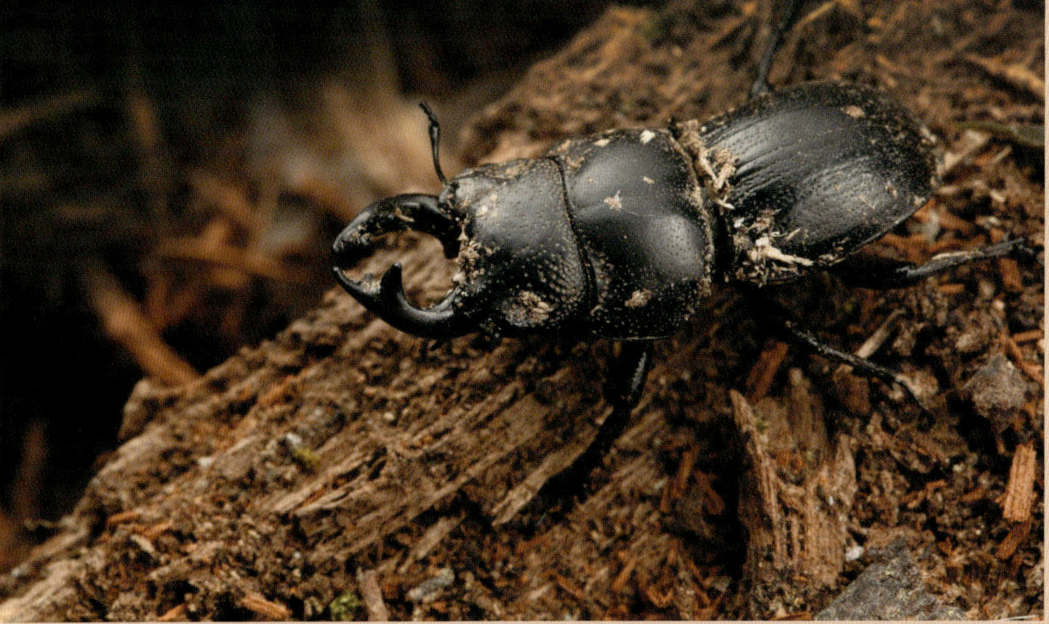

Lord Howe Island Stick Insect

Dryococelus australis

For 80 years, this large black stick insect was thought to be extinct. The fate of the Lord Howe Island stick insect seemed doomed by the accidental introduction of rats to its island home. But there was one place where the rats could not go: Ball's Pyramid. This volcanic sea-stack off the coast of Lord Howe Island is nearly inaccessible, but a couple of adventurous climbers ventured there to summit its steep peak. While there, they noticed a dead phasmid, but the survival of this species remained a rumour until an expedition was launched in 2001. It was then that a population of stick insects was found surviving on a single paperbark shrub. A second expedition with Melbourne Zoo then secured a pair of the stick insects to begin a captive breeding program.

Today, rodent eradication on Lord Howe Island and the successful breeding of its stick insect give the species a bright future, but it has yet to be reintroduced to the island.

Words and photograph: Jessa Thurman.

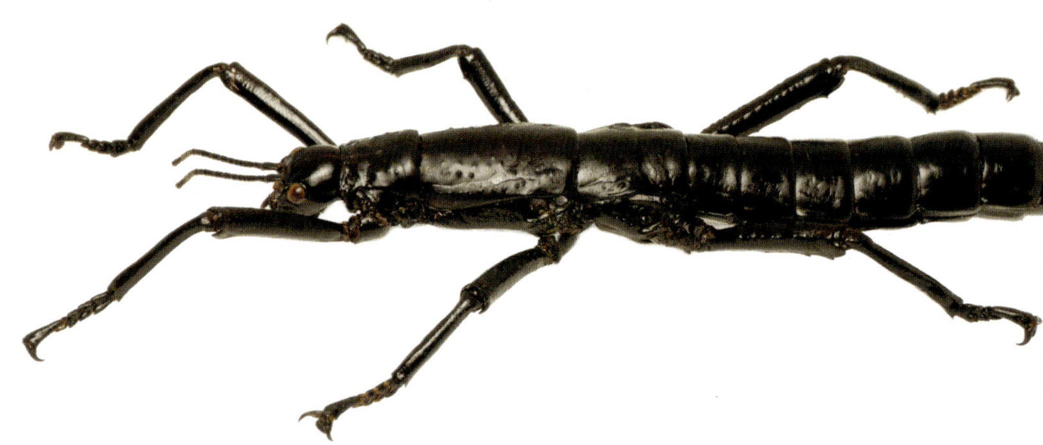

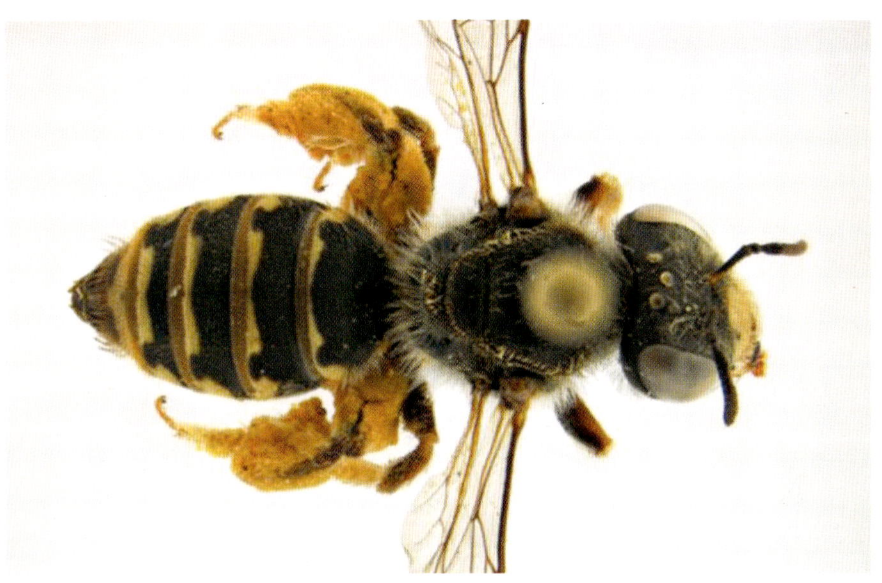

Short-Tongued Native Bee

Neopasiphae simplicior

While this bee was once found in a couple of locations, it is now only known from Forrestdale Lake Nature Reserve in Western Australia. The potential loss of this second population has alerted scientists to the risks that this species faces. This Critically Endangered native bee depends on the small patch of habitat it has left. To help it, we can protect its current habitat and create new reserves like it. We can also combat climate change, to reduce the intensity and frequency of unmanaged bushfires that threaten this species' habitat.

Words: Jessa Thurman.
Photograph: Museums Victoria.

Lord Howe Island Abalone

Haliotis rubiginosa

The Lord Howe Abalone is a small, 5cm-long gastropod that inhabits calcium carbonate boulders and rubble in the intertidal and shallow subtidal reefs of Lord Howe Island. Due to its small population size, density and distribution, this species faces a high risk of extinction from a range of threats including marine pollution (such as an oil spill event) and climate change. It has been assessed as Critically Endangered by the IUCN.

Globally, abalone are under threat from multiple impacts, including overfishing for meat and shells, diseases which spread rapidly through populations, habitat destruction, and climate change. Marine heatwaves can also compromise their immunity, making them more susceptible to diseases, and ocean acidification can reduce the survival rate of juveniles by dissolving their shells. **Words and photograph: Justin Gilligan.**

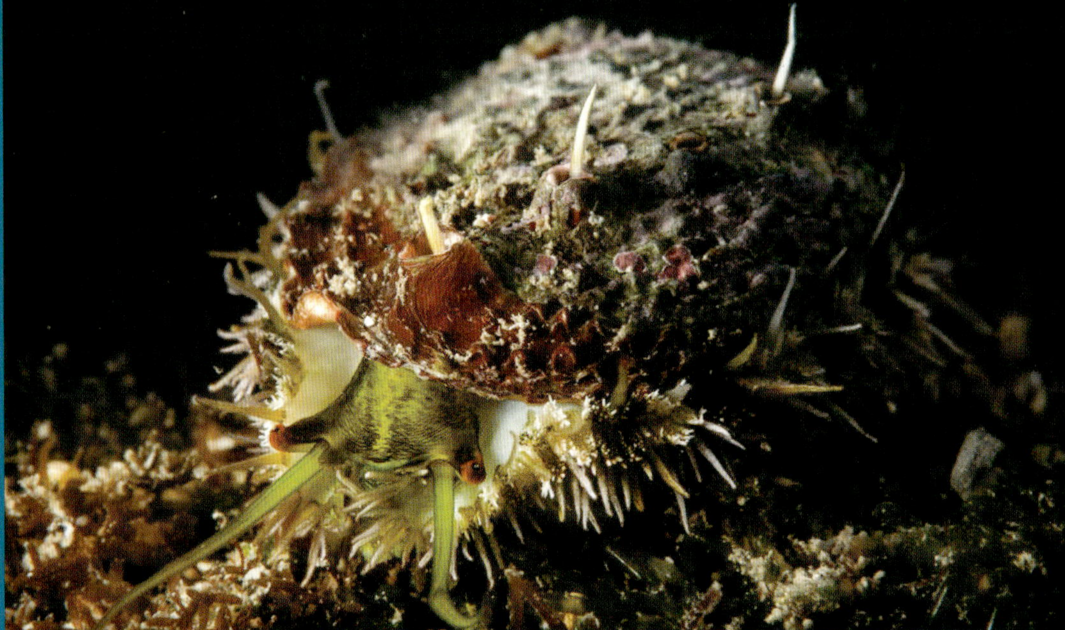

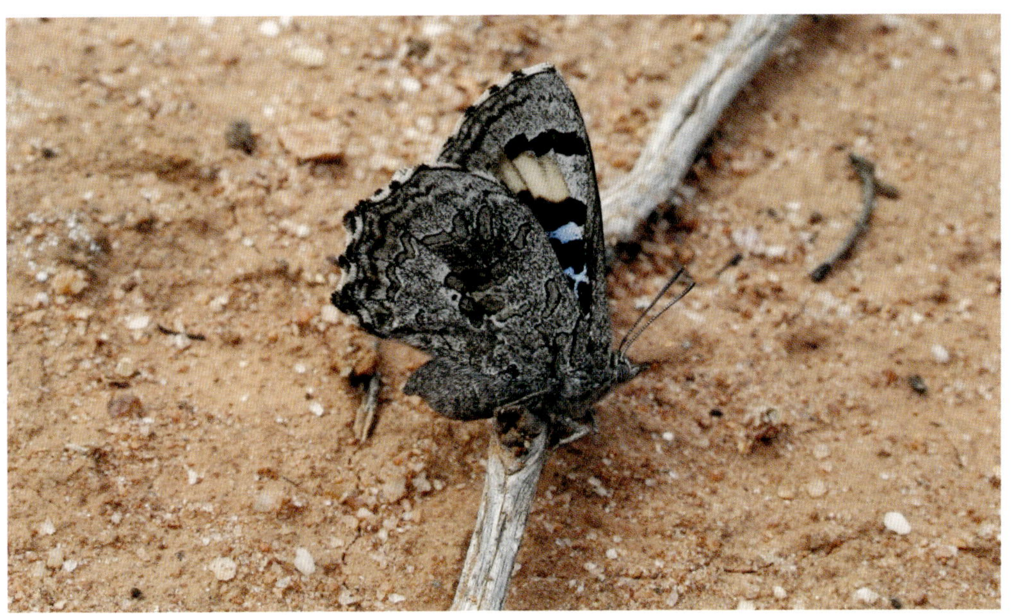

Arid Bronze Azure Butterfly

Ogyris subterrestris petrina

This butterfly is a rare jewel in the semi-arid regions of South Australia. Males butterflies can be seen flying rapidly and forming groups to attract females. Once mated, females will venture to the entrance of a sugar ant (*Camponotus terebrans*) nest, where she will lay her eggs. The ants take care of the caterpillars of this butterfly, and may be rewarded with sugary secretions for their service.

Only large colonies of sugar ants can support this species, restricting the butterfly to habitats that support the ants. This butterfly species has gone Extinct in New South Wales, with a Critically Endangered subspecies in Western Australia.

Words: Jessa Thurman.
Photograph: Andy Williams.

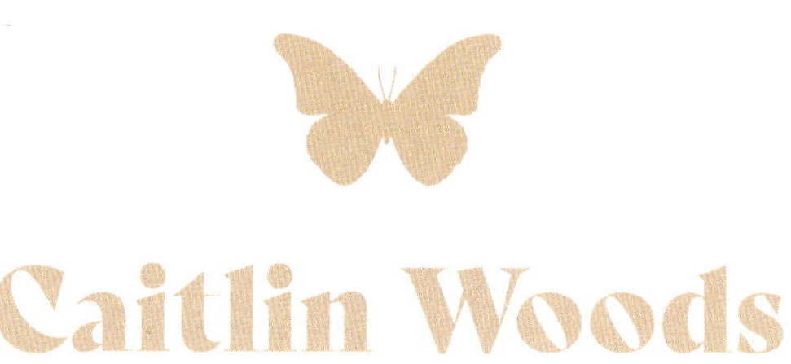

Caitlin Woods

PhD candidate

To me, invertebrates – animals without backbones – epitomise the wonder of nature. They are endlessly complex, intriguing, and beautiful, and their worlds offer more delight, fascination and inspiration than could be known in a single human lifetime.

Invertebrates are estimated to account for around 97-99 per cent of animal biodiversity – the overwhelming majority in our kingdom. Yet, being less familiar to us, their conservation lags abysmally behind that of the relatively few species with backbones (vertebrates). Efforts to assess and address threats to invertebrates are critical to conserve not only the immense biodiversity they represent, but also the earth's environments and vertebrate species, which they sustain by performing essential functions within all ecosystems.

> *Their worlds offer more delight, fascination and inspiration than could be known in a single human lifetime.*

On the World Heritage-listed Lord Howe Island, there are countless invertebrates which live only in this tiny, remote location. This makes them wonderfully unique, but also vulnerable to extinction. For example, there are Critically Endangered land snails which occur only on the summits of two volcanic mountains on this island. These species were driven to the brink of extinction after rats were introduced. However, thanks to a world-class rodent eradication program, this threat has now been removed and there are early signs of population recovery in some species.

Unfortunately, many endemic marine invertebrates are at risk of extinction, but few are officially listed as Threatened. The conservation status of less than one per cent of the world's invertebrate species is known, due to a lack of information about them.

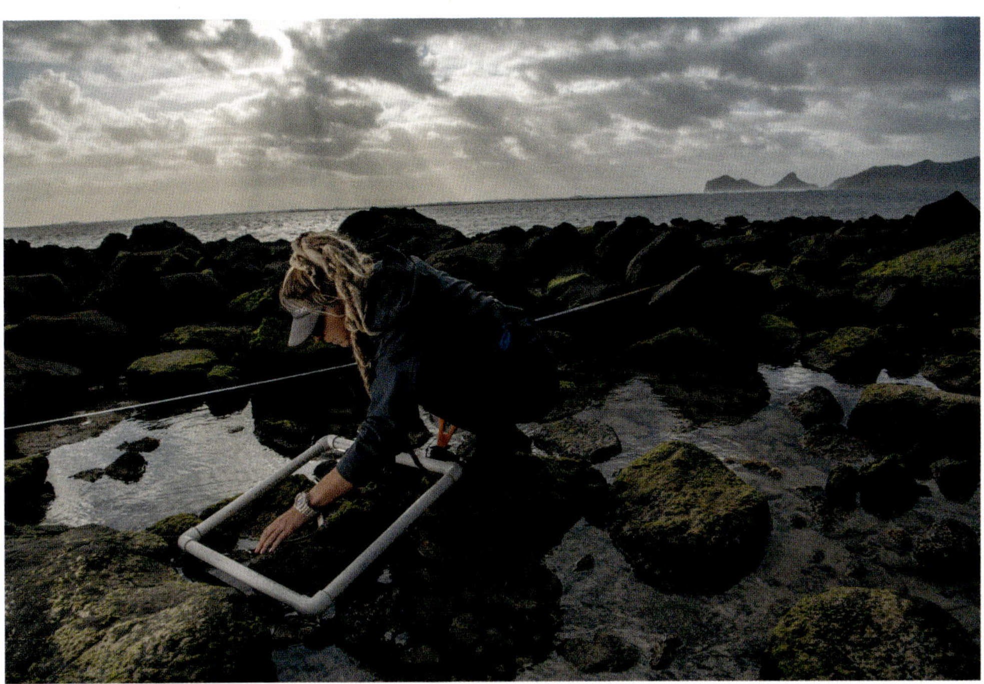

As a result, the effort put into invertebrate conservation is inverse to the proportion of biodiversity they represent.

Overcoming this begins with the fundamental job of describing, naming, and identifying different species – known as taxonomy. With such a vast myriad of invertebrates, it requires a great deal of dedication, attention to detail, and highly specialised expertise. This extraordinary work is a beautiful thing in itself – the painstaking devotion of one species to the intimate understanding of another despite being so different.

But without taxonomy, we cannot know what the true status of biodiversity is – whether it is changing, and which species are under threat, let alone identifying what those threats are and how to address them. This knowledge is stifled by a lack of support and funding for the taxonomic work underpinning it. Therefore, encouraging invertebrate taxonomy is one of the best ways we can help protect these minibeasts. We can do this by supporting museums, nurturing in ourselves and others a fascination and awareness of invertebrates, promoting education and projects, and fostering serious pursuits of these interests by the current and future invertebrate taxonomists the world desperately needs.

Photograph: Justin Gilligan.

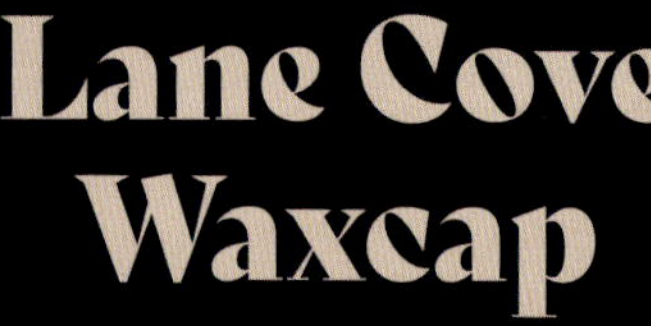

Lane Cove Waxcap

Hygrocybe lanecovensis

This beautiful species from the family *Hygrophoraceae* (common name: waxcaps) was discovered by Elma and Ray Kearney in June 1998, growing in a bushland leaf litter in North Sydney. Described by taxonomic mycologist Dr Tony Young, this rare species of waxcap assemblage was listed as Endangered by the NSW Scientific Committee in 2000, then as Critically Endangered in 2014. This species is threatened by fertilisers,trampling, smothering by creeper vines, toxins including herbicides, insecticides and diesel, as well as bushland mismanagement.

Words and photograph: Elma and Ray Kearney.

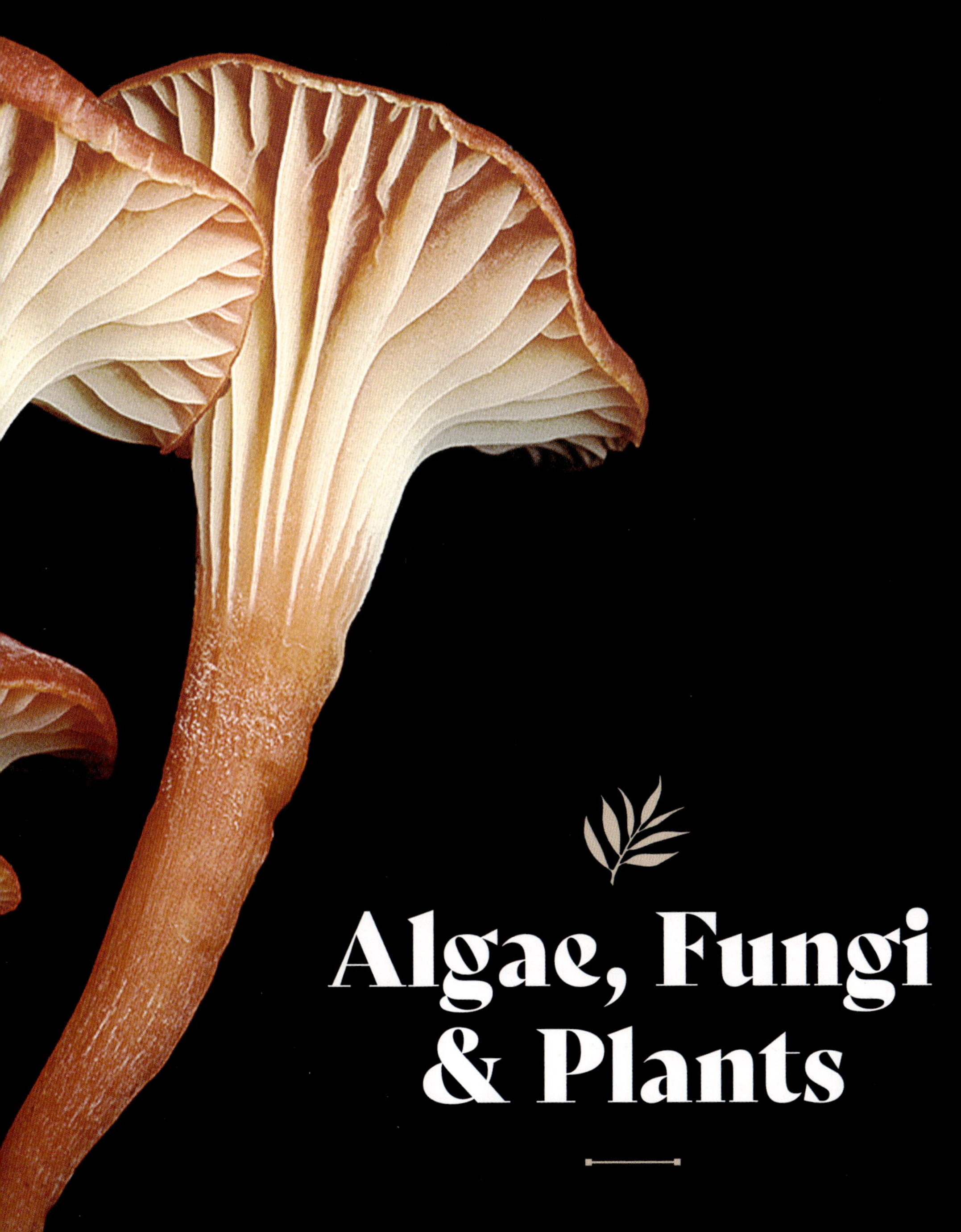

Algae, Fungi & Plants

Crimson Spider Orchid

Caladenia concolor

This beautiful terrestrial orchid grows to only 15-25cm high, but it has striking deep crimson flowers with petals up to 4.5cm long. It is restricted to just a few small populations growing in southern NSW and Victoria. The species survives the heat of summer as a dormant tuber, producing a single hairy leaf in autumn and a single stem bearing one or two flowers in spring. The flowers are pollinated by a single species of a nectar-foraging wasp, and the resulting dust-like seeds require the presence of a mycorrhizal fungus from the genus *Serendipita* to germinate.

Staff at the Royal Botanic Gardens Victoria have developed techniques to germinate the seed with the necessary fungus, and have produced hundreds of plants that will be used to reintroduce the species to appropriate habitats in the wild.

Words: Dr Karen Sommerville.
Photograph: Gavin Phillips/DPIE.

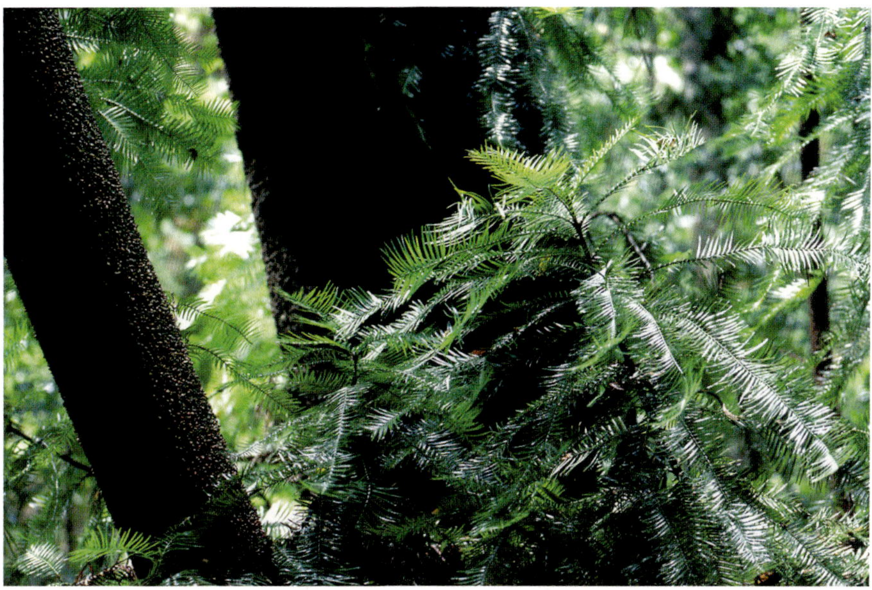

Wollemi Pine

Wollemia nobilis

The discovery of this species in 1994 caused a worldwide sensation. Considered to be a relic of the dinosaur age, the Wollemi pine is a conifer that grows up to 40m high and occurs only in remote canyons of Wollemi National Park, north-west of Sydney. To prevent enthusiasts collecting the species to extinction, the exact location of these populations is a tightly guarded secret.

Research on techniques to propagate the plant and develop an ex situ conservation collection began soon after it was found. This work led to the production of thousands of plants that were sold to the public (the first 148 were auctioned off by Sotheby's in 2005) with the proceeds funding ongoing work to conserve the species in the wild.

The Wollemi pine is now represented in botanic gardens and collections around the world. The original conservation collection, representing around 60 individuals from four populations, is still maintained by the Australian Botanic Garden Mount Annan, NSW. This collection has been an ongoing source of material for research to better understand the biology of the species, and has recently produced plants for translocation to the wild.

Words: Dr Karen Sommerville. Photograph: Jaime Plaza/Royal Botanic Gardens.

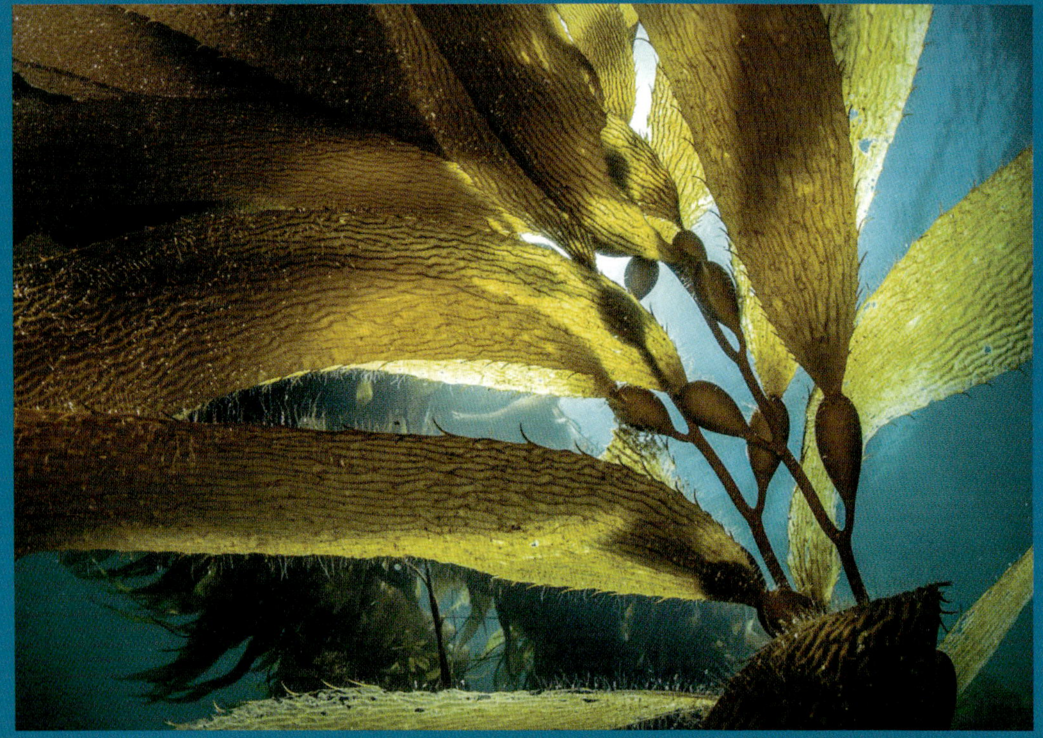

Giant Kelp

Macrocystis pyrifera

Tasmania was once home to vast forests of giant kelp, the world's largest and fastest-growing kelp species. Gas-bladder floats pull the plants up to 30m towards the surface, while at the base, the spindly tendrils of the root-like holdfast secure them to the sea floor.

The arrival of warm, low-nutrient water from the north weakened the giant kelp forests, making them more susceptible to storms, and eventually leading to their collapse across much of their former range in Tasmanian waters.

The warming water has also allowed long-spined sea urchins (*Centrostephanus rodgersii*) to extend their range into Tasmanian waters – they're herbivorous and feed on the kelp. By analysing historic aerial photography, a study documented a 95 per cent loss in Tasmanian waters between the 1940s and 2011.

Words and photograph: Justin Gilligan.

Tranquility Mintbush

Prostanthera askania

This aromatic shrub grows to 2.5m tall, and is known from just 11 populations on the NSW Central Coast. This plant mainly inhabits rainforest and wet eucalypt forest, and is threatened by urban development, weed invasion and altered fire regimes.

Representatives of Forestry Corp NSW, local government, landholders, the National Parks and Wildlife Service and the NSW Rural Fire Service have teamed up with NSW Threatened Species Officers to protect this plant at four sites. It is hoped that controlling weeds (such as lantana) at those sites, identifying the best fire regime to encourage recruitment, and working with landholders, will allow the species to flourish. Seed collections for this species are held at the Australian PlantBank and the Australian National Botanic Garden.

Words: Dr Karen Sommerville.
Photograph: Edwina Richards.

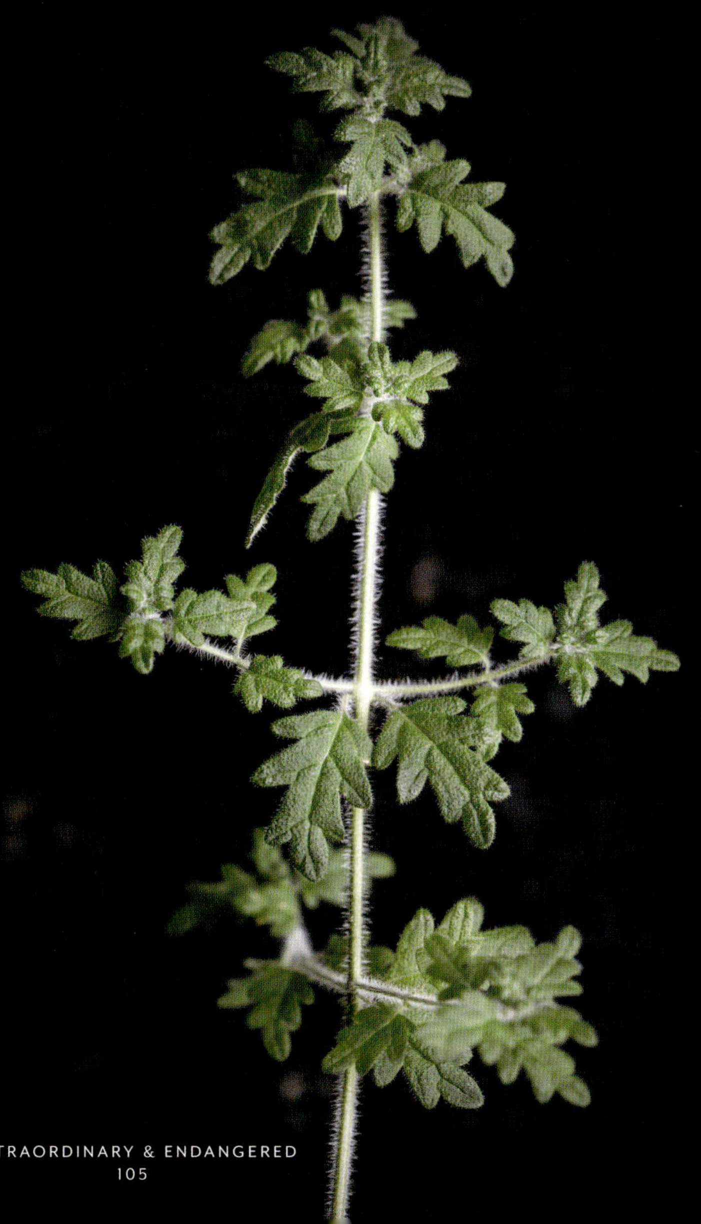

Small Purple Pea

Swainsona recta

This perennial herb is known for its beautiful flowers. This species was once widespread in the grassy understorey of woodlands and open forests in NSW, the ACT and Victoria, but is now restricted to just 26 sites. Studies show the smallest populations are prone to inbreeding; low levels of genetic diversity can lead to poor survival in any offspring produced.

One project to conserve this species resulted in the banking of multiple collections of seed at the Australian National Botanic Garden, and the propagation of plants for translocation to an offset site.

Local farmers near Queanbeyan, who stumbled on a population of the species, have worked with NSW Threatened Species Officers to erect fencing to protect those plants. Meanwhile, staff working for John Holland Rail have helped to protect plants growing along a railway easement by controlling erosion.

Words: Dr Karen Sommerville.
Photograph: SoS NSW.

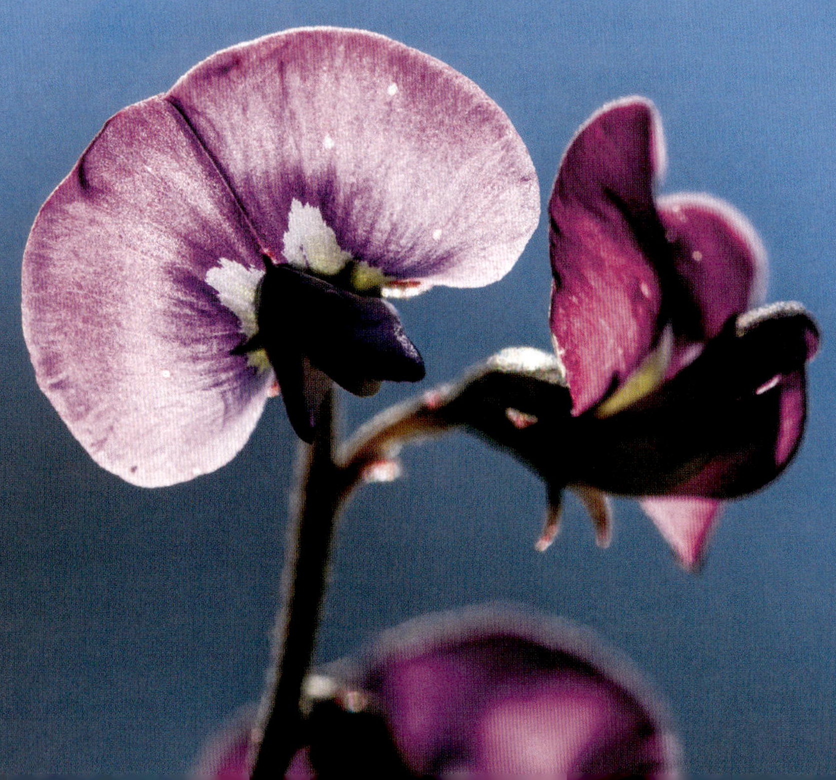

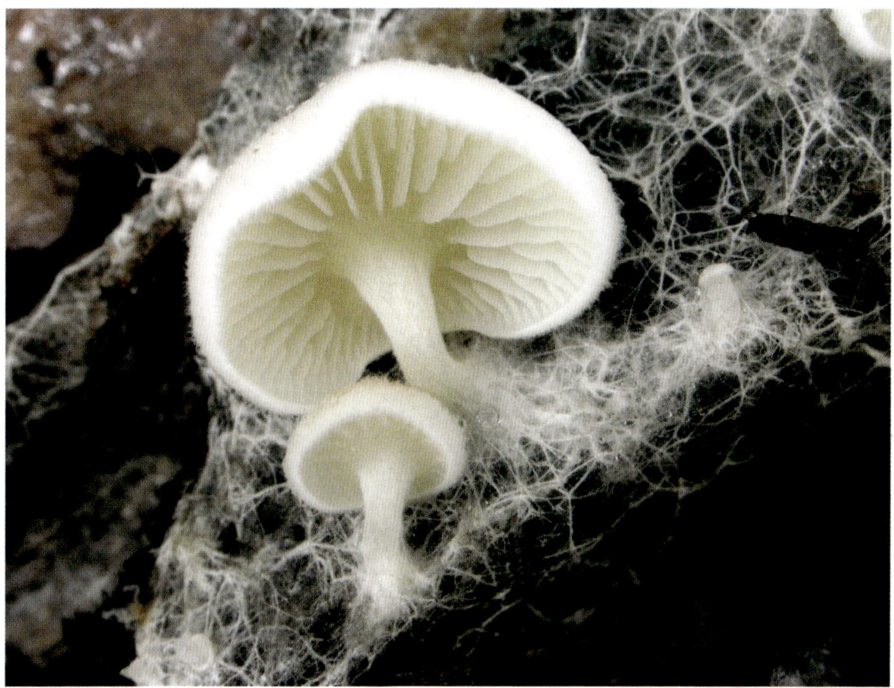

Hidden Pinkgill

Entoloma ravinense

The pure white fans of this little fungus grow on the inside surfaces of damp, rotten bark shed from the sugar gum *Eucalyptus cladocalyx*. Their woolly caps lie flat against the bark; some have short curving stems, others are stemless. The white gills gain a pink tinge as their spores mature.

Discovered in June 2010, three years after severe bushfires, it is known from only two places in Flinders Chase, Kangaroo Island. In spite of intensive searching, fewer than 40 fruit-bodies have been found, and none after the devastating fires of 2019 and 2020.

Although this fungus may need a suitable fire regime for the sugar gums to shed their bark, it is feared the recent fires may have destroyed the spore bank. Only continued searches will reveal whether this very rare fungus has survived. It has been listed as Endangered by the IUCN.

Words and photograph: Pamela and David Catcheside.

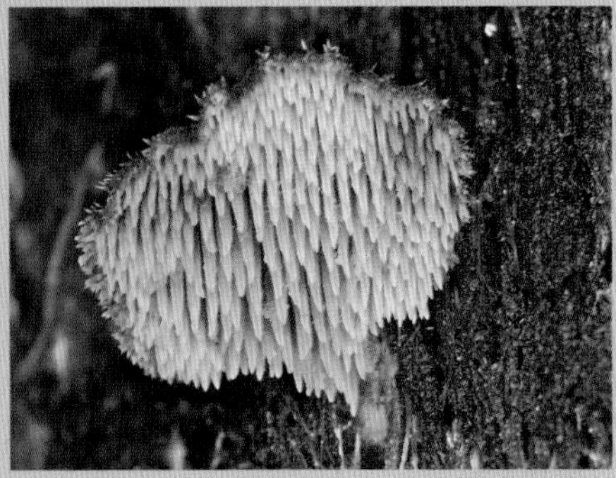

Stemless Earpick Fungus

Auriscalpium sp. 'Blackwood'

This inconspicuous fungus was first found in 2005, by members of the Field Naturalists Club of Victoria, and is an example of the vast diversity still yet to be documented among Australian fungi. Stemless earpick produces spores on spines on the underside of a shelf-like sporing body, which arises from the thick bark of large stringybark or peppermint eucalypts. It is known from only a few sites in central Victoria, on trees that have not been burnt recently.

It is regarded as Endangered due to its small population size. Increases in the severity and intensity of fire associated with global warming threaten the fungi that rely on long unburnt forests. Setting up spore banks for fungi, following the lead of seed banks for plants, will be important to secure the survival of species like stemless earpick and to allow for reintroduction if needed.

Words: Tom May.
Photograph: Jurrie Hubregtse.

Black Shoe Leather

Antrelloides atroceracea

Resembling small cushion-like lumps of discarded black shoe leather, this disc fungus grows with its base buried in sandy or lateritic soil. When dug out, it is seen to be top-shaped, with waxy grey, knobbly columns radiating upwards and outwards, and covered with a black layer containing spore-bearing sacs called asci. The name *Antrelloides* means 'like a little cavern', owing to the way this fungus has columns of stalactites and stalagmites gathered at its base, and is capped by a domed black lid. The chambered base with its above-ground lid is a very unusual form.

The lifestyle of this fungus, whether it is mycorrhizal forming symbiotic relationships with plants or a saprotrophic recycler, is unknown. Found only on Kangaroo Island in South Australia, and a sandy area in Western Australia, it has been assessed as Vulnerable by the IUCN.

Words and photograph: Pamela and David Catcheside.

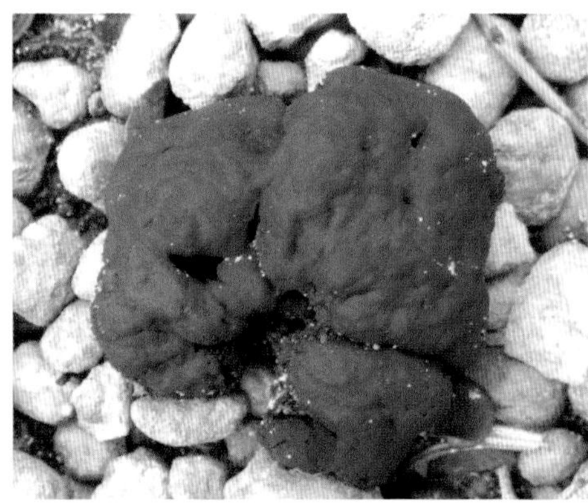

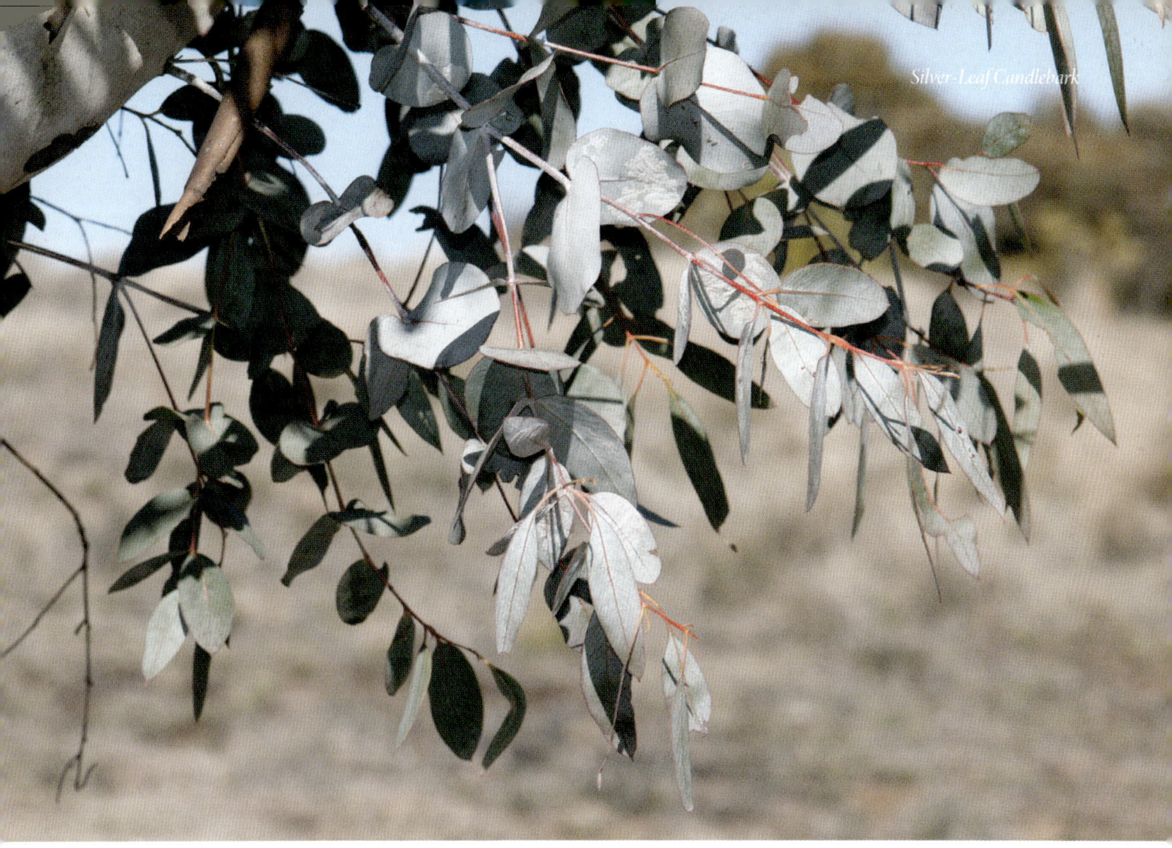

Silver-Leaf Candlebark

Eucalyptus canobolensis

The silver-leaf candlebark is a medium-sized tree that grows only on Mount Canobolas in the NSW Central Tablelands, chiefly at elevations above 1100m.

This beautiful tree is threatened by infestations of blackberry, which hinder regeneration from seed and increase the intensity of wildfires. Global warming is also expected to cause a contraction of the already limited distribution of this species, and may increase the impact of fires.

NSW Threatened Species Officers and National Parks staff are working to protect the trees in their habitat by controlling weeds, ensuring appropriate fire management, and monitoring the impacts of climate change.

A collection of 5000 seeds from trees near the summit of Mount Canobolas is stored at the Australian PlantBank, to provide insurance against extinction.

Words: Dr Karen Sommerville.
Photograph: Andrew Orme/DPIE.

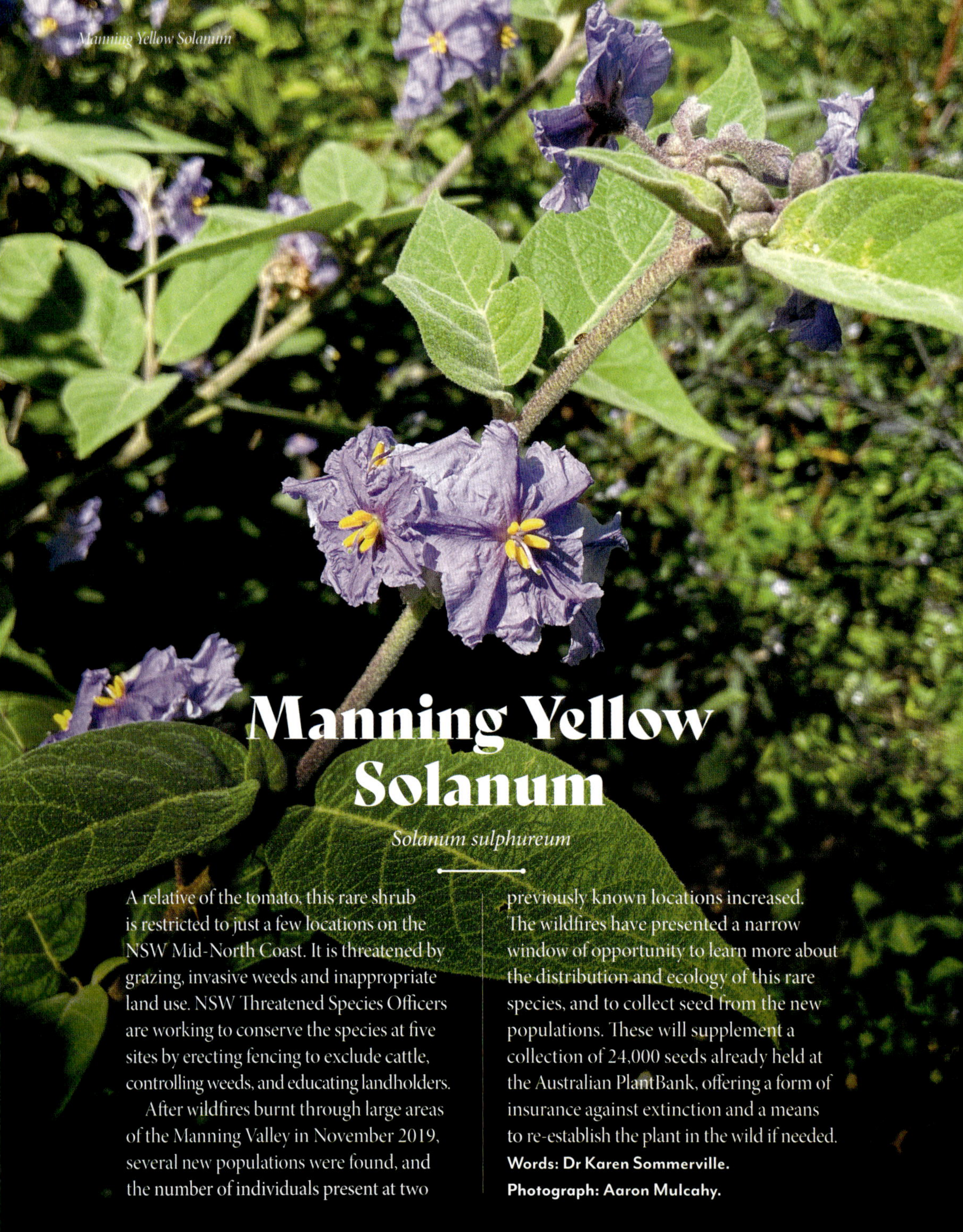

Manning Yellow Solanum

Solanum sulphureum

A relative of the tomato, this rare shrub is restricted to just a few locations on the NSW Mid-North Coast. It is threatened by grazing, invasive weeds and inappropriate land use. NSW Threatened Species Officers are working to conserve the species at five sites by erecting fencing to exclude cattle, controlling weeds, and educating landholders.

After wildfires burnt through large areas of the Manning Valley in November 2019, several new populations were found, and the number of individuals present at two previously known locations increased. The wildfires have presented a narrow window of opportunity to learn more about the distribution and ecology of this rare species, and to collect seed from the new populations. These will supplement a collection of 24,000 seeds already held at the Australian PlantBank, offering a form of insurance against extinction and a means to re-establish the plant in the wild if needed.

Words: Dr Karen Sommerville.

Photograph: Aaron Mulcahy.

Mount Dangar Wattle

Acacia dangarensis

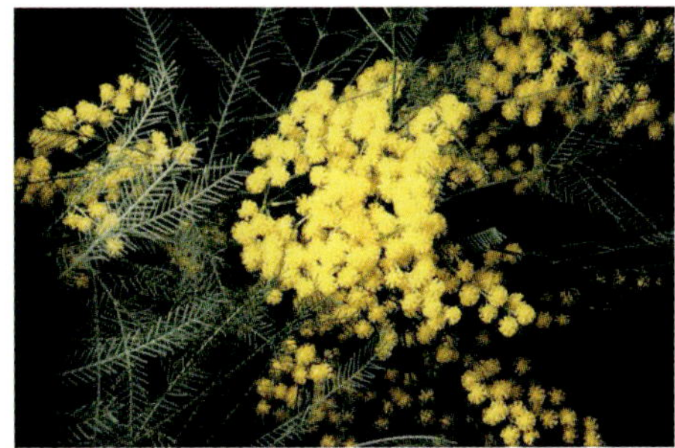

This long-lived small tree produces sprays of golden-yellow flowers. It grows only on the summit and slopes of Mount Dangar in Goulburn River National Park, NSW, and its very restricted distribution means the species is at risk from chance events such as severe fires and storms. It is also threatened by lack of recruitment, weed infestations (especially prickly pear), and grazing by goats.

NSW Threatened Species Officers are improving the wattle's chance of survival by controlling prickly pear on Mount Dangar. Two large collections of seed gathered in 2010 are held at the Australian PlantBank to provide insurance against extinction, and a source of material to re-establish the species in the wild if required.

Words: Dr Karen Sommerville. Photograph: The Royal Botanic Gardens & Domain Trust.

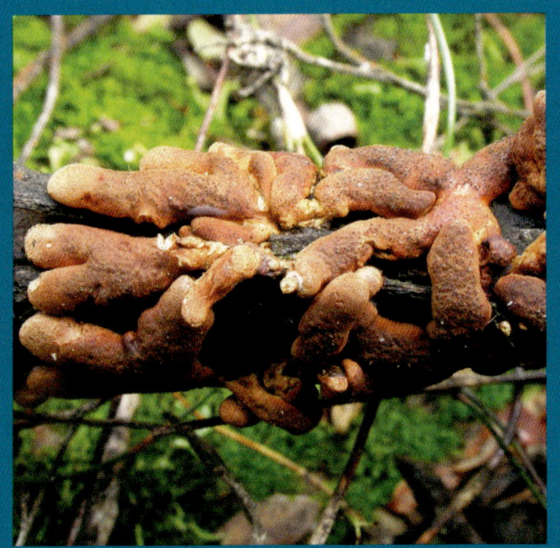

Tea-Tree Fingers

Hypocreopsis amplectens

This species produces brown, crust-like sporing bodies with finger-like lobes that clasp woody branches – hence the name tea-tree fingers. It appears to be a parasite on another fungus – a flat 'paint fungus' in the genus *Hymenochaete*. This in turn is a wood-rotter, decaying dead branches of various woody plants, including tea-tree and paperbark, that are understorey shrubs.

Tea-tree fingers is known from a couple of sites in New Zealand, southern Victoria around Western Port, and to the east of Melbourne, near the Yarra River. The worldwide population is estimated to be no more than 400 individuals, and the species is globally assessed as Critically Endangered. For the Australian populations, land-clearing has significantly reduced suitable habitat.

Words: Tom May and Michael Amor. Photograph: Tom May/Royal Botanic Gardens Victoria.

Wee Jasper Grevillea

Grevillea iaspicula

This small- to medium-sized shrub grows on rocky limestone outcrops and is found only in the Wee Jasper-Burrinjuck area north-west of Canberra. It is chiefly threatened by grazing, weed invasion, altered land use and fire. It also has very low genetic diversity and poor gene flow among populations, suggesting that it's unlikely to survive in the wild in the long-term without artificial enhancement of the populations. NSW Threatened Species Officers have built fences to exclude stock, planted more individuals within those fenced areas, and are controlling weeds. Seeds for this species are held at the Australian National Botanic Garden and the Australian PlantBank.

Words: Dr Karen Sommerville.

Photograph: Gavin Phillips/DPIE.

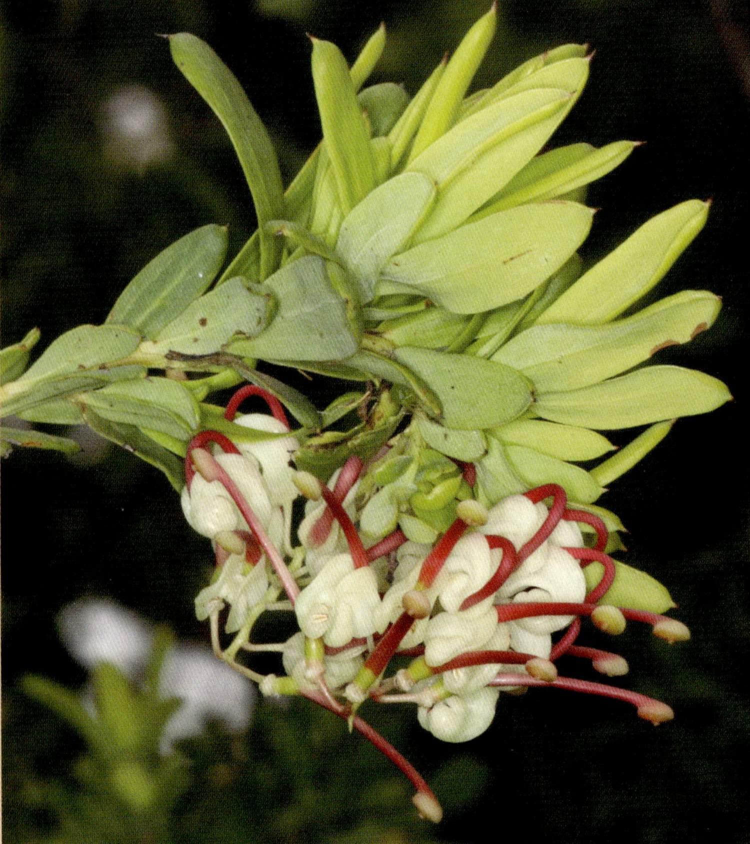

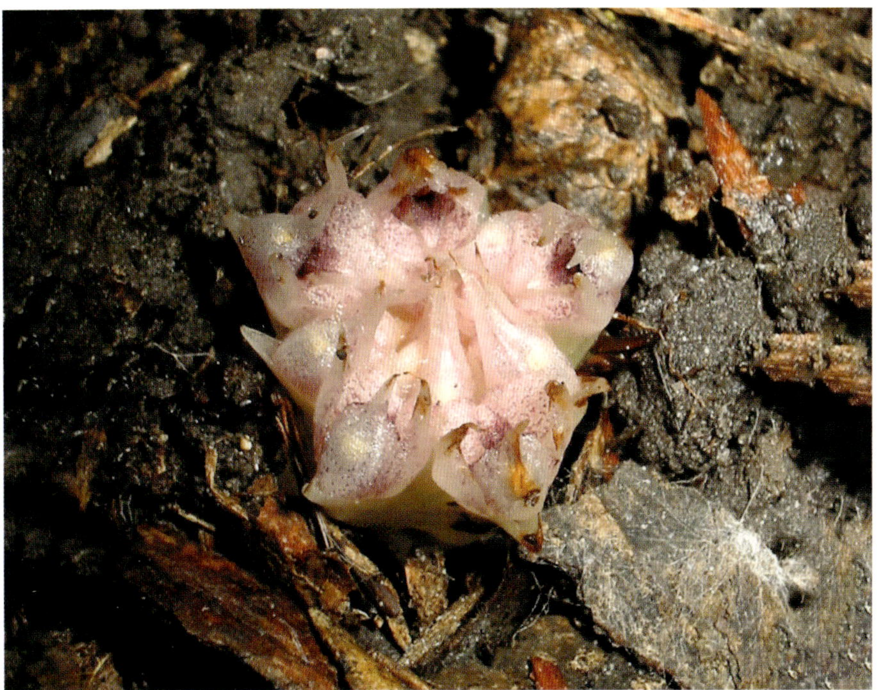

Underground Orchid

Rhizanthella slateri

First discovered in Bulahdelah, NSW, in 1931, this is one of five species of underground orchids, all endemic to Australia. This species is known from less than 10 locations, and is threatened by habitat loss, fires, and illegal collecting.

It spends most of its life underground, with only the flowers emerging just above the soil surface in spring. Since it has no access to the sun, it can't photosynthesise, and instead obtains sugars from other plants via a mycorrhizal fungus. Most orchids produce tiny, dust-like seeds that are dispersed by wind, but the seeds of *R. slateri* are larger than poppy seeds and are thought to be dispersed by bandicoots. As with other orchids, however, a mycorrhizal fungus must be present for the seeds to germinate.

Staff at the Australian PlantBank recently isolated this essential fungus and are now attempting to identify suitable plant species to support both the fungus and the orchid seedlings. If successful, any plants produced will supplement existing populations, and will also be used to train detection dogs to help find additional orchid populations.

Words: Dr Karen Sommerville.
Photograph: Lachlan Copeland.

Karen Sommerville

Research Scientist at the Australian PlantBank

My name is Karen Sommerville and I'm a Research Scientist at the Australian PlantBank. PlantBank is a conservation and research facility that sits within the Australian Botanic Garden in south-western Sydney. At the heart of the building we have a seed bank that holds millions of seeds. This seed bank is like the Global Seed Vault at Svalbard but, where the Global Seed Vault conserves the world's crop species, the focus of PlantBank is to conserve wild plants. At the moment, we hold seed collections for over 5000 Australian native species – if any of those were to disappear from the wild, we could withdraw their seeds from storage, germinate them, and return the plants to their natural habitat.

Our lives are very much dependent on plants. They produce the oxygen we need to breathe, and the food we need to eat.

Seed banking – storing dry seeds at sub-zero temperatures – is a great option for preserving plants from extinction and supporting their conservation in the wild. Some plants, though, have characteristics that make them difficult to bank. They might respond poorly to drying or freezing; they might be very difficult to germinate, or they might not produce seeds at all. These plants are the focus of my research. I work with a team of colleagues to collect fresh seeds from the wild, work out the best way to germinate them, then see how well they germinate after drying and freezer storage. We also look at alternative ways to conserve species that aren't suitable for

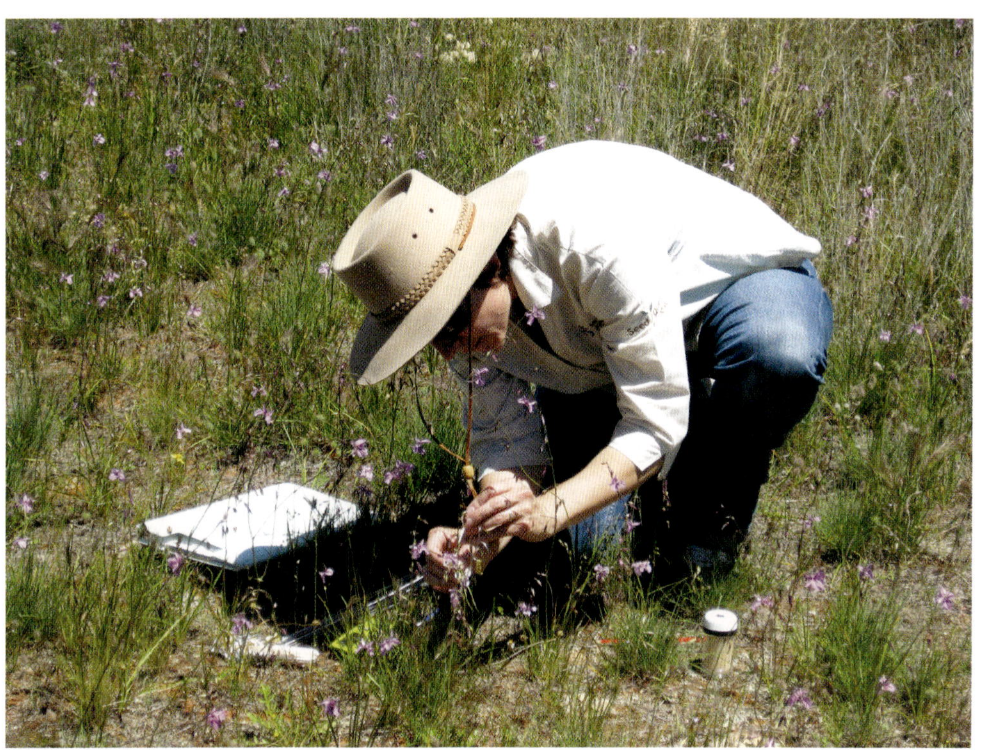

standard seed banking, which might include growing them in potted collections or tissue culture, or storing them in liquid nitrogen. This research has taken me from saltmarshes in Sydney to herb fields in the Australian Alps, subtropical rainforest in northern NSW, and tropical cloud forest in Far North Queensland. I've worked with seeds that are so tiny they need to associate with a fungus to germinate, and seeds that are so large they fill the palm of my hand. Australia has such a wonderful diversity of plants, that this work is endlessly fascinating.

Our lives are very much dependent on plants. They produce the oxygen we need to breathe, and the food we need to eat. They provide materials for shelter, fuel and medicines, protect soil from erosion, filter pollutants, and provide food and shelter for wildlife. Plants such as the ones described in this book contribute to the unique character of our landscape, and provide a home for our equally unique animals. These plants are well worth protecting, and I feel privileged to be able to contribute to their conservation.

Photograph: Matt Cameron.

Closing Statement

I remember during my undergraduate training, learning many marvellous things about the living world. All of them interested me. From the tiniest molecules of DNA that contain the instructions for all life on earth, to cells that form and fuse together to create new lifeforms, or those that divide and replicate en masse to build complex organs. Or – a particular favourite – the complex physiology that allows a giraffe to bow its head from lofty heights in order to drink without its head exploding from the sudden change in blood pressure.

But the part I loved the most was always learning about the end products of all that underlying biology – the organisms themselves. Millions of years of evolution leading to the incredible diversity of plants, animals, fungi, algae and microscopic organisms we see today. Endless subtle changes and iterations to better adapt to environments, hidden away in ancestors long gone apart from an occasional glimpse into the past through the fossil record.

This is biodiversity, and it holds the key to life as we know it. Yet, in my short lifetime, I have also had the unfortunate distinction to bear witness to an unfolding biodiversity crisis. Species extinctions within my very own, recent, living memory.

The Christmas Island pipistrelle, a type of bat, lost in 2009 likely due to invasive predators. In 2016, the Bramble Cay melomys, a native rodent, declared the first mammal extinction due to anthropogenic climate change. In 2017, again on Christmas Island, a small forest skink scurried from existence – the first Australian reptile extinction observed since colonisation.

What about the animals I study – frogs? I remember being captivated learning about Australia's incredible and unique amphibian biodiversity. From frogs that raise their offspring in a pair of 'hip-pockets' (p 74) or convert their stomachs into makeshift wombs (p 77), to others that burrow deep underground for years at a time to survive Australia's harsh arid interior, or those that have large tusks protruding from their jaw for fighting rival males.

Unfortunately, these have not escaped the impending crisis. The incredible gastric-brooding frogs of northern Queensland hopped from existence in the 1970s and '80s due to an invasive fungal disease, taking with them one of life's most remarkable reproductive strategies. Others, such as the

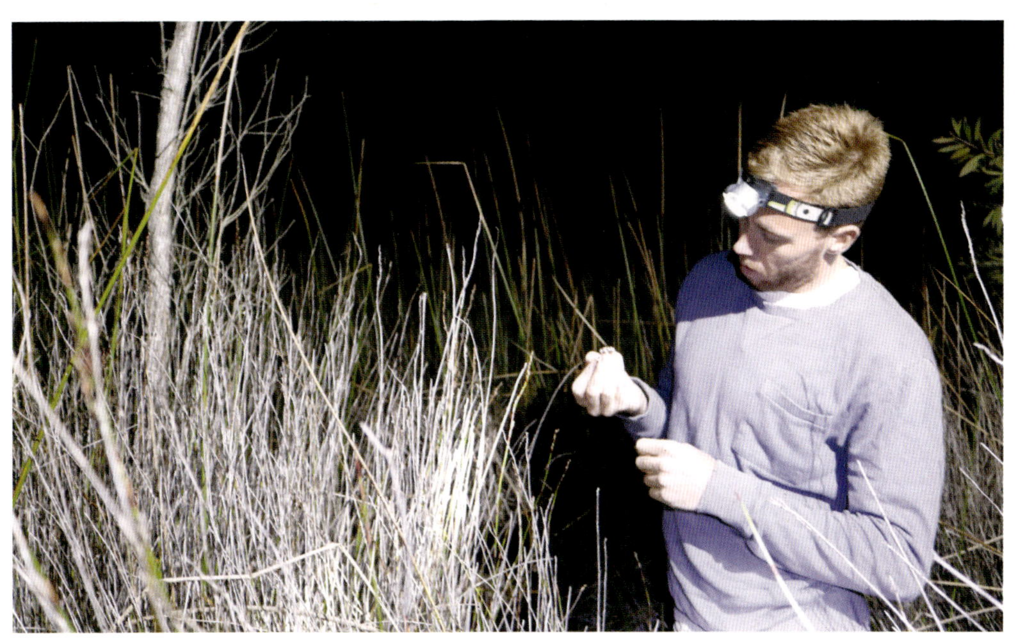

sharp-snouted day frog, suffered a similar fate. The striking northern corroboree frog from the snowfields of Kosciusko National Park has been reduced to about 50 animals in the wild, and could be the next to go. It is estimated that 50 per cent of all amphibians on earth are at risk of extinction.

It is easy to feel lost in all this gloom and doom. But I am a conservation optimist. As rare as they might be, we do have successes. We are developing ways of harnessing biological mismatch in environmental tolerances between frogs and the chytrid fungus killing them to create environmental refuges from the disease. We are developing ways to create disease-resistant frogs and reintroducing them to former habitats.

Others are working on ways to eradicate invasive species that affect so many of our native plants and animals by exploiting chinks in their biological armour. And despite our politicians' best efforts to ignore them, people are demanding action on climate change in order to change the course of history. There are solutions out there waiting to be found. Glimmers of hope.

I hope to see this conservation optimism spread. The problems can be overwhelming at times. But the truth is that we can all help. We can be proactive in lobbying those in charge to make positive change. We can all make a difference.

Dr Simon Clulow
Conservation Ecologist
Centre for Conservation Ecology & Genomics
University of Canberra

Australian Geographic

Extraordinary & Endangered

First published in 2022

Australian Geographic
52-54 Turner Street,
Redfern, NSW 2016
editorial@ausgeo.com.au
australiangeographic.com.au

Editor **Martine Allars**
Chief Sub-Editor **Serene Conneeley**
Sub-Editor **Rachelle Mackintosh**
Creative Director **Mike Ellott**
Senior Designer **Mel Tiyce**

Australian Geographic
Managing Director **Jo Runciman**
Editor-in-Chief **Chrissie Goldrick**
Commercial Manager **Simone Aquilina**
saquilina@australiangeographic.com

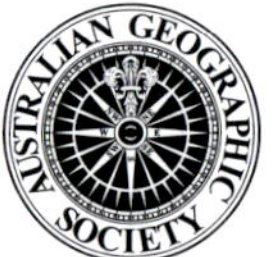

The Australian Geographic Society was established to encourage the spirit of discovery and adventure, and to foster love for our natural heritage. The Society and the Australian Geographic journal sponsor scientific research and conservation, and a portion of the profits from our published products goes back into the Society. Become a member today by subscribing to the Australian Geographic journal.

Subscribe now 1300 555 176
or australiangeographic.com.au
ISBN 978-1-92238-846-9

Printed by Leo Paper Group.

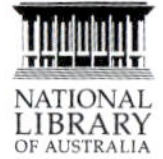

A catalogue record for this book is available from the National Library of Australia

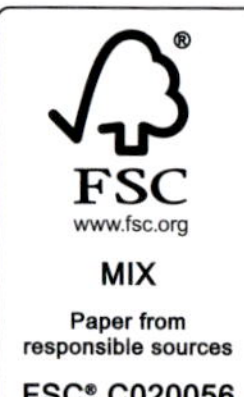

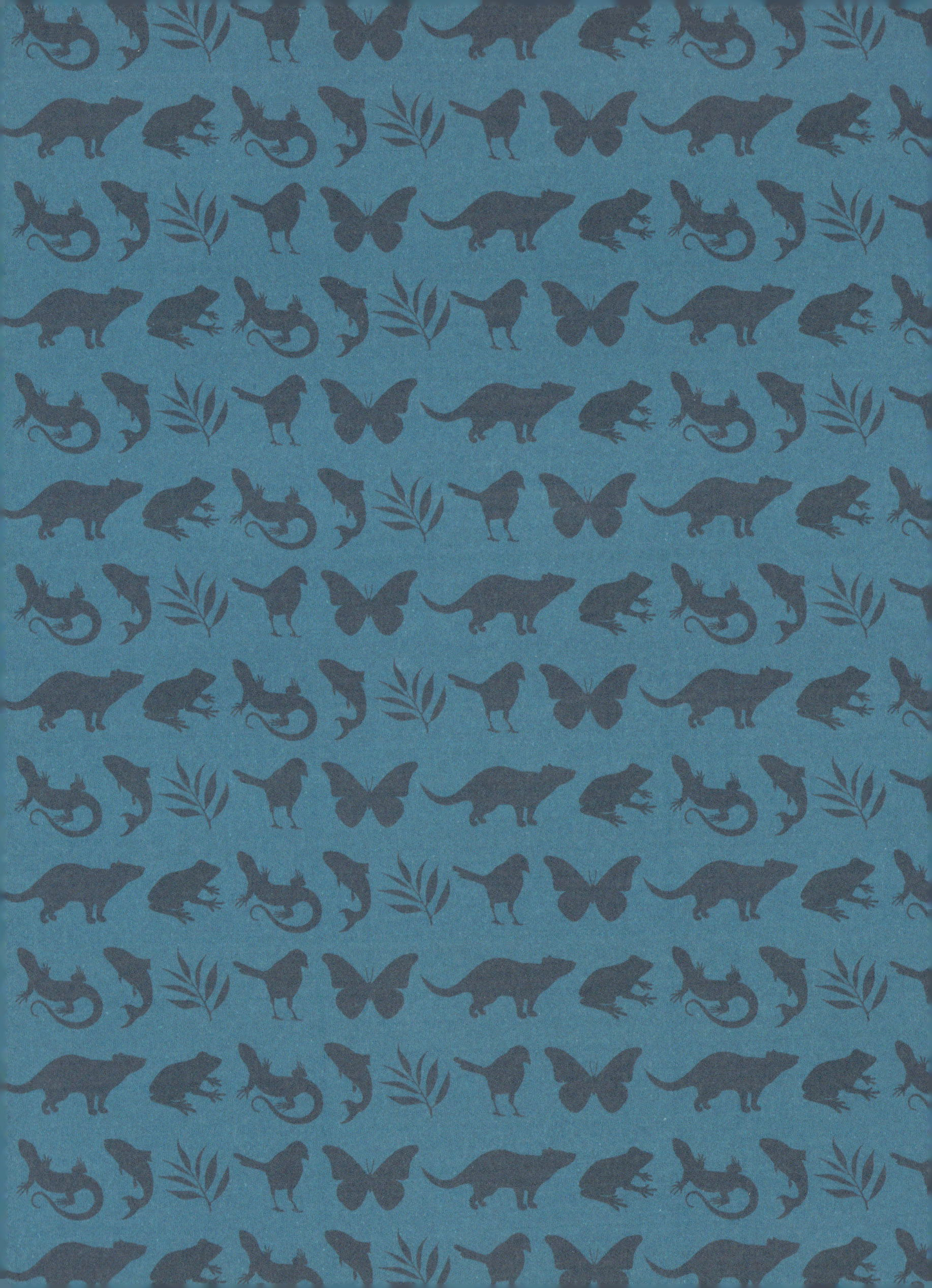